Here's anot... ....

you to dance with me

Carlosmanwelly

R.O.A.R

Here's another chance for you to dance with me

First Edition: 2024

Cover design by Sion Benney & Emma Galleti
with a little help from Craig Chapman.
Pictures from author's collection.

For my mother and my Aunty Anne.

Together again and forever in our thoughts.

XXX

And a massive shout out to

Blodwen, Sam, Marley & Finley

Acknowledgements

First of all, I want to thank my wife for having to listen to me go on and on about "my book", for enduring every chapter and verse, and for making sure I didn't mention anything or anyone I shouldn't; although I think I may have messed up on the anything I shouldn't bit.

I'd also like to thank anyone I have ever sent samples of my chapters. You've given me good feedback, encouragement, and honest critique; I really appreciate it. There are not many people I would ask so if you were one of them, it meant that I valued your feedback and was eager to hear your thoughts.

And, of course, to all my family for embracing the inner and outer weirdo in me.

And thank you to everyone I met during the rave days that I danced with, talked shit to, laughed with and spent time with; this book wouldn't have been possible without you lot.

I also want to thank all my followers and new friends that I've met on TikTok, Facebook, and Instagram, for their encouragement, advice, and kind comments.

And to Róisín Moriarty my proofreader for being on the same page as me from the get go: rtmproofreading.weebly.com

Last but not least, thank you to Rob for letting me tell just a tiny bit of your life's journey. I have always told you that you have a much more interesting story to tell than I have and one day I would love to read that book.

Contents

Foreword

When I first ventured into the world of raving in 1991, it was like stepping into another dimension. This book is all about my raving days; the mad times and adventures we had in that small space of time when unity, freedom, and self-expression were the name of the game.

It didn't matter who you were or where you came from; all that mattered was the music, the energy, and the experience we all shared. It was a time when strangers became friends and all boundaries disappeared in a field, a warehouse or an old railway tunnel.

For me, the rave scene and everything that came with it turned my life around when I wasn't in a good place mentally. It wasn't just about the partying; it was all the stuff that happened in between as well. 1991 to 1993 was an absolutely bonkers time for me.

This book is for you and for me. It's a look back at a time when the rave scene brought so many of us together in ways that we could never have imagined.

Although my raving days are behind me, the memories remain. While I still have those memories, I wanted to share them with you. I can guarantee that if you were there, you would have some wicked memories and stories to tell too.

1

I hope these pages give you a glimpse into a time when life was lived to the full, when the only questions that mattered were, "What's your name? Where you from? And what have you done?".

By the way

Some names and places have been changed to protect the guilty. Therefore, I have had to use a bit of creative licence to tell these stories.

"There will always be a reason why you meet people. Either you need them to change your life or you're the one that will change theirs."
Madeline Sheehan.

About Me

"The house of ill repute," my neighbours called it, but they had it all wrong. There was no ill reputing going on in my house although, from the outside, I could easily see why they might have come to that conclusion. A lot of people would come and go all hours of the day and night, by car and on foot. Occasionally, a transit van full of people would pull up outside, some of them would be scantily clad, and all of them were raving mad, so yes, I completely understood why my neighbours thought there was all sorts of crazy shit happening behind my closed doors and smoky net curtains, but there was no naughtiness going on at all. It was the house of peace, love, unity, and respect (PLUR). We lived as one Family.

But before I get into all the raving stuff, I think it's important to tell you a little bit about myself and my back story. Don't worry, I won't go into too much detail; it's just an overview to help you understand where I was, where I came from, where I went, and where I ended up. It's not an excuse for my behaviour but it might be a contributing factor.

Anyway, I'd lived in my house on and off since I was ten years old; it was my family home. We had moved from Cardiff Docks to the valleys because my mother was a victim of domestic violence or, as it was called in those days, a "battered woman." The man she had married, not my real father, by the way, used to beat her up and was violent to us as well. His favourite weapon of choice was his belt on us kids and his fists and feet on my mother. I vividly remember one night when my mother woke us all up screaming, "I've killed him, I've killed him." We all went into the bedroom to look, and there he was, lying in bed with a big kitchen knife in his chest. It was wobbling, so it wasn't in that deep. He looked over at us and said, "Look what she's done to me; she tried to kill me."

I was gutted he wasn't dead. None of us said it to each other but I think we all thought the same thing. After that, my mother threw him out of the house; it wasn't the first or last time. A few days later I was walking around the shopping centre with my friends and I spotted him. He called me over and opened his jacket to show me a knife; the same knife that'd been wobbling in his chest. He looked at me and said, "Tell your mother this is for her." Another thing he used to do was make us eat porridge with salt instead of sugar. He said it was the traditional way to eat porridge and it was the way his mother used to make it for him; it was fucking disgusting. As kids, all we wanted was sugar and more sugar. Fucking salt in porridge? By fuck!

He was also obsessed with us peeing the bed (I was still watering my sheets on a nightly basis up until the age of ten). Whenever he came home drunk from the pub, he would check if we peed the bed and if we had, he'd wake us up and belt us. The stupid fucker thought that by giving us the belt it would stop us from doing it but it had the opposite effect; we'd go to bed terrified and end up peeing with fright.

My aunty and my mother's friends convinced her to go to Women's Aid. They helped us run away a few times. We lived in hotels, hostels, and women's refuges with other families. But he would always end up finding us and beg my mother to take him back, feeding her full of shit and false promises. He'd tell her things would be different this time but they never were. That happened quite a few times; I lost count of how many primary schools I attended. I've still got girlfriends from some of them; I never got to say goodbye or finish with them. We never knew when we had to leave or were going to leave; one day, we would be in one school and the next, we would enrol somewhere different. I think that's how I learned to make friends so quickly and lose them quickly as well. Eventually, the people in Women's Aid said they had to move us out of Cardiff, somewhere he wouldn't be able to find us. My mother didn't want to move out of Cardiff; all our family was there, and it's where she was born and bred. But she was battered and beaten, and realised it was the best thing to do for all of us so that's what happened. They moved us deep into the heart of the Welsh Valleys, where no fucker could find us, and I have to say that was the best thing that ever happened to my mother and us.

I think if I'd stayed in Cardiff, I probably would have ended up in prison. My best friend at the time was always getting into trouble and sometimes I would go along with him because he was a good laugh. I remember one time when we moved back to Cardiff, I went to visit him; he said he was running away from home and he asked me if I wanted to go with him. I had no reason to run away but I said yes because I hadn't seen him for ages. So we ran away together, and it was the worst two nights of my life. We broke into garden sheds so we could sleep in them, and I remember being so hungry that I pinched an apple from the display outside a greengrocer's shop. I was so happy when our mothers eventually found us. He ended up in and out of prison later on in life and there's a high probability that I would have too. So I am incredibly grateful for everything they did for us at Women's Aid; not only us but many other families.

My family consisted of my mother and my four siblings. There was an older and younger brother, an older and younger sister, and me in the middle. My real father was what's known these days as an "absent father". I would see him when I was out playing sometimes; we would always chat and he'd give me ten pence to go and buy some sweets, but that's about it. Occasionally, I would see him passing the school while I was in the playground. I would run along the side of the fence, talking to him until the fence ended and became a stone wall, so I couldn't see him anymore, but he would always give me ten pence before the fence ran out. My mother liked him, and my gran and aunty did, too; they told me he was always laughing like me and he would ask how I was when they saw him in town.

After a while, my mother met a man who eventually became her boyfriend, and we all moved in with him. He's mentioned a few times in this book so I'll refer to him as my stepfather, even though they weren't married; it's easier than saying "my mother's boyfriend" every time. It wasn't all plain sailing and they had their ups and downs, but he wasn't violent to us kids or our mother so it was much better than what we were used to. We moved back to Cardiff a few times and to other places around the valleys, but we would always end up back where I eventually called home.

In 1988, when things seemed to be settling down and we hadn't moved for a long time, my mother was diagnosed with lung cancer and on April 18th 1989 at the age of 42, she passed away. I was seventeen at the time. A few weeks before she died, we were planning what to do for my eighteenth birthday party. It was a really tough and harrowing time for us all but I still had my aunty and my gran in Cardiff and all my cousins. My aunty stepped up for my mother and became our mother. She looked out for us. She would call up to see us whenever she could, and we would call down to Cardiff to visit her and to see all my cousins and my gran. I would write letters to my aunty all the time; she had nine children of her own, so we couldn't exactly move in with her, but she was only a phone call away and was always there if we needed anything. She never missed one birthday or Christmas card for any of us; sometimes, that birthday card was a godsend because she would always put a fiver in it. I would borrow money from people based on it. There was one time I didn't have any food in the house and woke up on my birthday starving. I laid in bed, waiting for the postman to arrive, and sure enough, he delivered a card from my aunty with a fiver in it. I went straight to the post office and bought some pasties; I loved the pasties from the post office.

After my mother passed away, I expected my father to come looking for me to see if there was anything I needed or to check if I was okay. I knew my aunty and gran used to see him when they were shopping so they would have told him about my mother, but he never did. I was gutted about that; I could have done with ten pence.

I left school without any qualifications so I had to join the Youth Training Scheme (YTS) with a load of my other mates; the headers from school who didn't have any qualifications or work skills either. We each had to pick a trade to learn; either bricklaying, carpentry, or painting and decorating. I chose painting and decorating because I didn't like the thought of working outside and I was no good with my hands; I'm not a very practical person. I enjoyed my time on the YTS. A gang of us were sent to an old church with a supervisor to look after us. We painted the same walls over and over again for a year, and I learned how to clean paint brushes properly. I made some good contacts on the YTS for all sorts of dodgy stuff but I got sacked in the end for missing too many days. When my supervisor called me into his office to tell me, I cried like a baby. I didn't beg him for my job back or anything like that; I don't think I cared about losing my job. I don't know why I cried but I felt stupid afterwards. But by then, I was old enough to sign on—I was entitled to £67.20 a fortnight—so that's exactly what I did.

Anyway, about a year after my mother passed away, my younger brother and sister moved out of the house and out of the village to live with my older sister. Then my older brother moved in with his girlfriend in another village and my stepfather moved in with his new girlfriend in a different part of the same village. That is how, at 18, I ended up living on my own in a three-bedroom terraced house. Well, not exactly on my own; I did have Rip, my trusty little mongrel, who I will tell you all about in a bit.

My House at the Bottom of the Street

It was a terraced house on a relatively quiet street where everybody knew everybody's business. Most of the people who lived on the street were old couples. Four doors down from my house was the post office, where I used to cash my giro and buy my pasties. On the opposite side of the road was the corner shop, where I used to buy my booze and fags, and sometimes, when I was really skint, I would sneak the odd box of frozen food and some toiletries under my jacket. There was a public phone box just around the corner from me. I used it as my personal telephone number because I didn't have a phone in my house, and there were always kids hanging around. If it rang, they would answer it, and if it was for me, they would knock on my door.

I liked my little terraced house. It had a tidy-sized living room with a Parkray coal fire that I had a love/hate relationship with. I loved it when it was lit and stayed lit but I hated it when it went out, and I had to light it, especially if I couldn't afford to buy coal; although sometimes I used to go up to the colliery with a little "piggy sack" and forage for coal around the surface. I lived in a coal mining village so there was an abundance of it around. Everybody used to do it, especially during the

Miners' Strike. I would also riddle the ashes to recycle the coal and, when times were really tough, I would go out into the back lane and riddle my neighbour's ashes that they threw out; other times, I just had to put up with no hot water and a cold house.

The living room was very dark because it had those brown wooden walls all around, tongue and groove, I think it's called. It was all the fashion back then. I had a decent three-piece suite; it had lots of blim holes in it from smoking joints but that added to its character. The carpet in the living room was tough wearing, thank fuck, like the ones you find in a Wetherspoons pub. I think it was an Axminster.

To the left of the living room was another little room we called "the parlour." It was more of a junk room but done out posh. There was a piano in there as well because my stepfather played the piano, and then on the right of my living room was the kitchen. It was a big kitchen but basic as fuck. There was a big fuck-off sliding glass door separating the living room from the kitchen that made a hell of a noise when it was opened and closed, and another coal fire in the kitchen, a Rayburn, that doubled up as a cooker with an oven and a hob. I didn't light the Rayburn often because I couldn't afford the coal to keep two fires going. Next to the kitchen was a door which led to a small utility cupboard, on the right was the back door to the garden, and straight in front was the bathroom and toilet, or the "brown room" as everyone called it because *everything* in it was brown; the oval-shaped bath, the toilet, sink, shower cubicle, even the tiles on the walls and floor—all brown.

There was no upstairs toilet or bathroom. When I first moved into the house, my stepfather gave us a bucket to take up to bed with us to pee in rather than have to walk all the way downstairs; apparently, it was the norm. I remember thinking, where the fuck have I moved to? It felt like I was back in the 1940s or something. We weren't allowed to shit in the bucket, and every morning we would have to bring it down to empty it into the toilet. But it was handy when I went through my drinking phase as a teenager because I used it as a sick bucket as well as a pee bucket.

There were three bedrooms upstairs; I had the biggest room at the front of the house, the one I used to share with my brothers, and the rest of the bedrooms were for whenever any of my family came back to stay over. I didn't have to pay any rent to my stepfather but he did expect me to pay all the other bills, like electricity, water rates, television licence and poll tax. I never paid any of them though because I wasn't really sure how to go about doing stuff like that. Besides, I was on the dole so I didn't have enough money to pay the bills anyway. They sent me loads of letters and bills but I just threw them on the fire. I also found out that I could claim housing benefit towards my rent payments, even though my stepfather didn't want any rent from me. But they didn't know that so I got an extra £60 a fortnight.

Anyway, as I said earlier, before I take you on the rest of my journey, there are still a few things I need to get out of the way first, so bear with me; it's all relevant, I promise you. I've never written a book before and I look at it a bit like baking a cake; you have to prepare all the ingredients before you start cooking, and I also need to warm the oven up a bit. I think you are the oven and this book is the food.

Two doors up from the corner shop and directly opposite my house, there was a guy living on his own. He was about twenty-five and would have parties in his house every weekend. When I was younger, I would stay up all night looking out the bedroom window at the antics going on outside his house. All the older boys we looked up to would go to his house, and they would be partying all night long. Sometimes, the women would fall over drunk outside, and I would catch a glimpse of their knickers; that was the main reason I would stay up all night. I vowed to myself that one day, I would have a house just like that. And a few years later, lo and behold, due to a series of extremely unfortunate events, I did have a house like that, as in there were lots of parties going on but without all the drunkenness and the girls falling over outside flashing their knickers. I suppose that could have happened but I never witnessed it myself.

Occasionally, my stepfather or my brother would move back into the house when they had argued with their girlfriends and got chucked out, which was always a pain in the arse because it would interrupt my routine. Whenever my stepfather moved back in he would always wake me up early and tell me that I needed to get a job and learn a trade. I would say to him there wasn't much work since Thatcher closed the mines. He hated Thatcher so that would start him off on one of his rants about how she had fucked the miners over and decimated the valleys, and he would forget about me needing to get a trade. There was one time he tried to wake me up early, but I was too fucked to get up so he left a note on the mantelpiece for me that read…

Clean up the bins outside; the neighbours are complaining about the mess. Most people dream with their eyes closed and some people dream with their eyes open.

I thought that was a loaded note; not the part about the bins, I knew I had to clean up the mess outside, but the "some people dream with their eyes open" bit. He was insinuating that I was a dreamer and living in a dream world; of course, he was right. He was only looking out for me but I did take it to heart a bit. He always told me I wore my heart on my sleeve; he used to say I was too sensitive and he was right about that.

Anyway, I sorted the bins out and left him a reply to his note that read...

I've cleaned the mess and sorted the bins. I may be living in a dream world, but I'm committing no sins.

When he came home later, I was still up. He read my note and laughed; he said he wasn't being sarcastic or having a go at me; he had seen the quote somewhere and thought I would like it. We ended up having a good chat; he was a clever bloke and I learned a lot from him. He used to tell me that I had a lot of potential and that if I put my mind to it, I could be anything I wanted to be, and it frustrated him that I was wasting it. I didn't know what potential he was on about, mind; I couldn't see fuck-all at that time in my life.

Anyway, that was my humble abode. I've still got a bit more ground to cover before I take you to the juicy bits. So, let's get on with it...

Rip

Now, let's get onto Rip, my trusty four-legged bestest friend in the whole wide world. Rip was my mother's dog but obviously our family dog. He was an Airedale terrier mixed with something else that I can never remember; he was a scruffy little black bugger… we were a lot alike.

He was a cheeky dog, full of character and funny as fuck. There were times when we would piss each other off because our personalities would clash. Now and then, he would rip up my trainers when I was in bed because we argued. I used to have to remember to hide them from him in the nights and sometimes I forgot. That used to really piss me off mind because I didn't have a lot of disposable income to go buying a new pair of daps. Sometimes, we wouldn't talk for a few days after he did it.

That's why we called him "Rip", because when we first had him as a puppy, he ripped up my mother's cigarette packet, and he continued ripping things up as he grew older. I suppose it was a case of if the cap fits, then wear it; which, in a way, was kind of what happened to me too.

The other thing he would do was shag the towels. He would pull them off the radiator or the bath, scrunch them up into a ball, to resemble another dog, I suppose, and then fuck them. I didn't have many towels back then either, so it was a bone of contention between us (pun intended). There were times when I accidentally dried my face with a towel that he had spunked all over, so that would cause arguments as well. But we'd always lick and make up. We used to have some really good chats; he was a good listener, and we were there for each other when the chips were down.

We would often go for long walks up the river or the woods. I would roll a few joints for the journey and we'd be out of the house for hours. He loved it when I threw him in the river; we had a favourite spot on the rocks where the water was deep but calm. I would throw him in, he would swim back out, climb up the rocks, and wait for me to pick him up and throw him in again. If he had his way, we would stay in that spot and do it all day. That's where we differed; he was much more daring than me and a good swimmer. He was an independent dog as well; he had his own friends and would sometimes wander off on his own to go exploring. My stepfather had taught him not to go after the sheep, so he didn't bother the farmers. He had his regular places and people he would visit, and there were times when I wouldn't see him for days, but I knew he was always okay because he was a streetwise dog; a tough little fucker too, who could take of himself in a scrap, and he knew all the good places to hang out for food.

There was one thing he used to do that was a bit strange though, but funny as fuck as well. I had this one friend I knew from school; for the purposes of this story, I'll call her Marcia. Anyway, Marcia would often call down to my house for a chat; we weren't boyfriend and girlfriend, just good friends. But as soon as Rip saw, heard or got a whiff of her, he would go nuts and shag the fuck out of her leg. He was like some sort of obsessed or possessed animal whenever it came to Marcia; I don't know what it was about her but he didn't do it to anybody else. It got to the point where I had to lock him in the kitchen before letting her in the house, and if I went to the toilet and accidentally left the sliding door open a little bit, he would nudge it open with his head, then pounce on her leg and hump away at it. I had to remove him from her leg forcibly, and that wasn't easy either because he would growl at me as he was grinding away. He was proper feral when it came to Marcia. If I put him out in the garden, he would run around to the front and wait for her outside the front door. I admired his tenacity for that, mind.

Whenever my stepfather came home drunk from the pub, he used to bang out tunes on the piano in the parlour; Rip would jump onto the piano and start howling as if he was trying to sing along. He'd throw his head back and howl like a werewolf; I used to feel pity for Gladys next door. We spent a lot of time together, me and "Ripper Roo", as we liked to call him. He was my soulmate.

Staying "In In"

An average day for me was getting up at about one o'clock in the afternoon, making some breakfast for me and Rip, and then settling down with a cup of tea and a fag to watch *Neighbours* on BBC One. I loved *Neighbours*; I never missed an episode and if I did sleep late for some reason, I could always catch the repeat at half past five. After *Neighbours* finished, I'd roll a joint if I had any blow and then put some music on. Sometimes, I'd put a tape on; other times, I'd watch MTV, depending on how I felt and what I wanted to listen to. Back then, my favourite albums to listen to were:

Pink Floyd – Any album,

Bob Marley – Legend

Big Audio Dynamite – This is Big Audio Dynamite

Jeff Wayne – The War of the Worlds

Roxy Music – Flesh and Blood

EEK-A-Mouse – Mixtape

Jean-Michel Jarre – Revolutions

London Beat – In the Blood

I also had *The Wall* on video and would watch that on repeat. I felt a lot like Pink in that film, having built a kind of wall around myself since my mother's death. I understood what it was like to be *Comfortably Numb*.

MTV was quite repetitive, but the songs and videos I liked were:

R.E.M – Losing my Religion.

Sinead O'Connor – Nothing Compares to you.

Lenny Kravitz – I Build This Garden for Us.

Neneh Cherry – Buffalo Stance.

MC Hammer – U Can't Touch This.

Vanilla Ice – Ice Ice Baby

I also started writing poems and odd stories; all very dark, depressing, and sad. I didn't know it at the time, but I was experiencing some sort of mental and nervous breakdown, and something told me to write it all down and get it out of my head. It was a "better out than in" kind of thing. I was grief-stricken and, although I had a family, I didn't have anybody to talk to about it; putting it into words helped lighten my load.

To give you an example of what I mean by *dark*, I'll show you one of the poems I wrote one night while sitting in the house, reflecting on my situation, my life, the universe and everything beyond. It's called *"The Key to Hell"*...

The key to hell

I've got the key to the room of hell
It's in my head and in yours as well
We are all in hell but in different stages
It's like a book, but we're on different pages
No two hells are both the same
You are judged by your character
and not by your   name
Our cards are marked we are heading for sin
In the end, it's the devil who'll win

I would hardly leave the house, except if I needed to go to the shop or sign on the dole. I did have one or two friends I would call on as well but I wouldn't go to pubs or clubs or anywhere near a lot of people or crowds. That's why I liked taking Rip for a walk up the mountain, out of the way; because I wouldn't see any fucker. If I weren't listening to music, I would look for comedy programmes on the TV. My favourite comedies were:

Mork & Mindy
Monty Python
Anything featuring Spike Milligan

Red Dwarf

If I wasn't watching comedy, I liked to watch Vietnam War films or period dramas; I still love a good period drama to this day. There would always be friends calling around my house for a smoke or a chat; it was nice to see them but also nice to see them go. I have always enjoyed my own company and I had Rip as well. I wasn't depressed, or I didn't think I was; I was just always deep in thought and had a lot of things to think about and to write about and to get out of my head.

Anyway, I think there are about two more small chapters before I get to the juicy raving parts. I hope I haven't bored you already, but I wanted to transport you into my world. The next two chapters are like a bridge from one world to the next, and without that bridge, I would never have crossed the river to the rave.

My Mate Simon and the Police Raid

Simon was my closest friend at the time; he would call down my house quite a lot, never in the day because he was working, but in the evenings and weekends if he wasn't with his girlfriend. I knew him from school but I didn't know him *in* school as he was a year older than me.

I'm not sure how we started hanging around with each other. All the women liked Simon; he was the typical, tall, dark and handsome type of guy, always well-dressed and properly preened. His footwear matched his clothes and he was confident. Some people called him "the catalogue kid" because he looked like one of those models in a catalogue but I never did; I thought it was a childish nickname.

He wasn't a talker like me; he was more of a listener but when he did speak, it was worth listening to what he had to say. He lived with his parents so that was the reason he would always be over my house. His girlfriend was at Manchester University, studying psychology, so he would visit her some weekends and stay up there, but she took her studying very seriously. He wasn't always allowed to see her because she was "revising", which I did think was a bit dodgy and sometimes I would tease him about it.

Anyway, the good thing about Simon was that he had a well-paid full-time job. He was a subcontractor and if anyone needed a road laid, in and around South Wales, he was the man who could organise it all. He never got his hands dirty but he knew how to bring the right people together to get the job done. He once offered me a job but from the way he explained it to me, it sounded like a lot of hard work, and it was outside work; I wasn't a fan of working outdoors. The reason it was good that he had a full-time job was because he wouldn't disturb my daily routine of watching *Neighbours* and writing and listening to music with Rip; it also meant that he always had dope on him because he received a wage packet every week, unlike me.

We would spend the weekends in my house getting stoned and drinking Thunderbird, and sometimes girls would call around because they knew he was in my house. The other good thing about him was that he had a driving licence, while I couldn't drive at all; I had never even sat in a driver's seat in a car. Simon had access to all sorts of vehicles—vans, cars, and trucks—so he was convenient for lifts and if I ever wanted anything shifted, like a sofa or a wardrobe. He often took me to Cardiff on a weekend to see my aunty and never charged me because he was pinching red diesel from work. He got on with Rip as well, and Rip liked him, although sometimes I would catch them arguing; he once said to me...

"Rip is a good dog, but he can be a bit of a prick sometimes."

I thought he was bang-on with that assumption but let's face it, we can all be a bit of a prick sometimes.

When it was magic mushroom season, we'd walk up the woods with Rip and pick some 'shrooms.' We'd sometimes keep them for later; other times we'd "pick and eat", and by the time we got back to my house, we'd be tripping our boxes off. I liked a mushroom trip, but I wouldn't take too many, only about fifty at a time, just enough to hallucinate and giggle. The first time I ever took them, I ate about a hundred, and I didn't really like the experience; the things I saw scared me a bit, but fifty or so was a perfect balance. At the time, they weren't illegal to take so everybody in the village would be tripping during mushroom season. Although it was illegal to freeze them, dry them out or make them into tea, we often did all three.

On that note, Simon was in my house the first time I ever got raided by the police. It was a Saturday night and not really a proper raid. They didn't bust the door down, thank fuck; they just knocked like anybody else, and when I answered it, as you can imagine, I was very surprised to see eight police officers on my doorstep, and a few more sat outside in cars and vans. Obviously, all my neighbours were out watching the drama....

"We've got a warrant to search your premises."

"Search my premises for what?"

"Illegal substances."

"What illegal substances?"

"Cannabis, but we'll take anything we can find."

And then they all just barged into my house. It was a good thing Rip was out at the time or he'd have gone mental on them; he didn't like people in uniform and wouldn't have taken too kindly to their attitude towards me either. As luck would have it, none of us had any dope on us; we had just put our last joint out and Simon was about to go and score, until we were rudely interrupted by the law.

So I wasn't worried about it. I knew they wouldn't find anything so I let them carry on, but then I remembered what was in the fridge—well, in the pull-down freezer compartment of the fridge, to be precise. There were roughly two hundred magic mushrooms in a box of Findus Crispy Pancakes; no crispy pancakes... just magic mushrooms. It was folded up so they couldn't see inside it but there was nothing else in the fridge, not even milk or butter. So I was very concerned about them finding the mushrooms… very concerned indeed.

The first thing they did was to search the both of us; they patted us down and then told us to empty our pockets. I did even better; I pulled my trousers down and took my pants off. I was going to bend over and pull the cheeks of my arse apart but I thought It was best not to provoke them too much. They searched the settee area where we were sitting and then emptied the contents of the ashtray into an evidence bag; we were instructed to sit down and shut up while they searched the rest of the house. I didn't put my trousers back on; it was my house. If I wanted to sit on my sofa naked, it was up to me, and I wanted them to feel uncomfortable, but I started to feel awkward sitting next to Simon with my cock out, so I got dressed.

After about five minutes of watching them jumping on my chairs with their shoes on and looking on top of cupboards, opening drawers in the kitchen and tipping stuff out, I thought fuck it, they can't tell me what to do in my own house, so I went into the kitchen to keep a keen eye on them. I watched as the sergeant opened the fridge door, and then he pulled down the freezer compartment and stared straight at a box of what he thought was Findus Crispy Pancakes. He turned around to me and said...

"Times are tough, are they, son?"

"What's that supposed to mean?"

He smirked at me.

"There's more food in Mother Hubbard's cupboard than in this house. I'd ask you for a cup of tea but you got no milk."

"I Blame Thatcher, the milk snatcher; she took it all."

He smirked at me, then closed the freezer compartment door and the fridge.

I smiled at him then, with a big sigh of relief, I went back to the living room to sit with Simon.

I whispered to him...

"They didn't find magi's,"

But then the sergeant called my name...

"Can you come here a minute and explain this to me?"

I thought he'd opened the fridge door again and looked inside, or he might have even planted something like they do in films. I walked into the kitchen, but I couldn't see him. He was looking in the cupboard next to the kitchen, the one full of my stepfather's tools and junk and WD40. He looked at me and said...

"What's that flashing blue light doing there?"

31

I looked in the cupboard. It was a blue light off a police car that my brother had brought home from fuck knows where and put it in the cupboard.

I turned to the sergeant and said...

"It's not flashing. It's just a blue light."

"You cheeky little bastard; think you're funny, do you? Where did you get that light from?"

"I don't know, I didn't even know it was in there."

"Well, it looks like it's been stolen from a police vehicle. Put him in the van, boys; he's coming with us for a little trip down to the station. And put that blue light in an evidence bag." Then one of the other coppers cuffed me and marched me out to the police van; shortly after that, they all left with the non-flashing blue light and the contents of the ashtray. They didn't arrest Simon; they told him he was free to go or stay. He stayed for a while and explained the situation to Rip when he came back.

I spent the night in the police cells and was released in the morning without charge. They told me that the contents of my ashtray were being sent to the laboratory to look for traces of cannabis and I would hear from them shortly on the findings. A few weeks later, I had a letter from the police informing me that no further action was being taken.

My Mate Rob and the Big Bang

Right, so now I've told you all about me, my family, my mate Simon, and Ripper Roo, as well as where I was mentally, physically and possibly metaphorically. It's time to tell you about Rob before we get onto the raving parts. Now, it's difficult to know where to start with Rob; anybody who knows or has ever met him will tell you the same thing. So, I'll start with a description of him:

Name: Rob

Age: 21

Height: 5'10

Weight: 10 stone

Ethnicity: Caucasian

Hair: Long, blond, sometimes tied into a ponytail

Eyes: Blue

Distinguishing Features: Crooked nose, a faded tattoo of a cross on the right arm

Modus Operandi: Typically targets small to mid-sized pubs in quiet or residential areas with minimal security. Prefers establishments with multiple gaming machines and accessible cash tills. Gains entry through back or side doors, often using basic lock-picking tools or crowbars. Heads directly to cash tills, cigarette machines and bandits.

Speed and Efficiency: Operates quickly, spending no more than 10-15 minutes in the building. Appears knowledgeable about pub layouts and often has a clean entry and exit plan.

Behavioural Patterns: Known to avoid confrontation, preferring empty establishments, not likely to engage if confronted. Non-violent.

Known Associates: David Harries, Colin Rees.

I had heard of Rob and, like Simon, we were in the same school. In fact, everybody in the village had heard of Rob. I had been in his company in the past but never spoke to him until, one day, he knocked on my door. He had a joint in his hand and said...

"Have you got a light, mate?"

It was a weekday but he was dressed like he was going to a nightclub; he had a pair of brown winkle-picker shoes, black stay-pressed trousers with a crease down the middle, and a white shirt buttoned up to the top. The reason I remember it was because I thought none of what he was wearing suited what I had heard about him. He looked odd as fuck and interesting to talk to, so I invited him in....

"Of course I have, as long as I can have a puff of that joint. Come in."

We got chatting, and he was nothing like people were saying; he was funny, down to earth, really easy to talk to, and always laughing after he said something. Rip liked him as well. I went to the kitchen to make a cup of tea and left him rolling another joint. When I brought the tea back, I noticed a big silver coin on the coffee table. It wasn't there before and certainly didn't belong to me. As I was about to sit down, Rob passed me the joint and asked if he could go to the toilet; I told him where it was and off he went. When I sat down, I took a closer look at the coin; it looked like one of those big chocolate coins you get in a Christmas stocking. I lifted it up for closer inspection, and it gave out a big BANG. I almost shat myself as I threw it across the room. I turned around and could hear Rob laughing his head off from the kitchen; then I laughed at what he must have seen. I thought, what kind of crazy fucker takes a joke coin out with him for a laugh, and I knew from that moment that we were going to get on really well.

Now, let me give you a bit of backstory about Rob to explain some of what I mentioned earlier about the pub thing. By the age of nine, he'd smoked his first cigarette, and by ten, he was addicted to nicotine and wouldn't go to bed unless he had a cigarette after his supper. By the time he reached his teens, he was out of control; back then, I think they would have called him a "juvenile delinquent." He was a rule breaker; if he was told not to do something, he wanted to do it even more.

This is why, at the age of fifteen, he ended up in a Detention Centre in Gloucestershire, otherwise known as "Borstal," after the town in Kent, where the first one was opened in 1902. They were prisons for naughty boys aged between 14 and 17 that the system deemed were out of control but too young for adult prisons. In the early Eighties, Thatcher re-branded Borstal as a "short, sharp shock", the aim being to rehabilitate young offenders and steer them away from a life of crime by enforcing harsh military discipline onto them and into them. Now, without getting too political, it didn't have the desired effect on the youth of yesterday. They were beaten, abused, humiliated, and made to feel like the scum of the earth by the guards. Even today, some are still suffering from what they endured. Countless stories have surfaced from those who went through the system and continue to grapple with the trauma of the so-called "short, sharp shock" treatment.

He once told me a story about one of the guards. He said he was walking down the corridor when a guard called him over and told him to run to the end, read the sign on the wall, and then run back to tell him what it said. The thing is, the guard already knew what the sign said, and so did Rob. But he had no choice—if he didn't do as he was told, he'd get a beating. So he ran to the end of the corridor, read the sign, and ran back to the guard. When the guard asked him what it said, Rob answered:

"No running in the corridor."

So the guard gave him a beating with a rubber hose for running in the corridor.

In his own words, he said to me one day:

"Carl, they turned me into a bullet; I was like a little soldier, the fittest I have ever been in my life. If they told me to do 150 press-ups, I knew if I didn't, they would kick fuck into me; at first, I couldn't, but then I quickly learned to do 150 press-ups and 100 more if they asked me to. What they should have done was send me straight to the army afterwards but they just put me back on the outside in the real world, and I was angry with them and angry at the system. One thing for sure: after being in that place, the police never caught me on foot again; I was too fast and fit for them, and I knew if I did end up going to prison, it could never be as bad as a Borstal was."

Not long after I started hanging out with Rob, my stepfather couldn't understand why I was friends with him. He had had a few dealings with him in the past, and none of them were good. He said to me one day…

"Carl, tell me what he has got on you and I can help. Do you owe him money?"

"No, it's nothing like that; he's a good laugh but people misunderstand him."

"Misunderstand? I understand exactly what he is and I'm telling you now, he's no good. And if you carry on bothering with that boy, you'll end up in prison with him."

Anyway, Rob was on the dole like me and he liked watching *Neighbours* as well, so he would be down my house nearly every day after that, just in time for it to start. He had his own flat but, like me, wasn't paying his bills so he was always getting evicted. He didn't have a driving licence but he occasionally borrowed a car from his brother or one of his mates; driving illegally was much easier back then.

Simon knew Rob as well, so we all got on. Sometimes, they would go out to the local pubs together but I would never go with them; they'd come back afterwards and have a few joints with me. Rob brought a good dynamic to my house and where Simon was quiet, Rob never shut up, and we'd have some really deep conversations; he was a lot more street-wise than me and had a "fuck it, why not?" attitude, whereas I had the "let's wait and see" attitude. We were kind of opposites to each other, even to look at but we met somewhere in the mid-dle, like a Venn diagram.

And now the stage has been carefully set. Let's get the party started and get onto the raving parts…

Our First Rave

Once upon a time on a Saturday afternoon, I was sitting in my house with Rip, watching MTV, when Rob and Simon called in and asked if I wanted to go to a party on a farm in West Wales. As per usual, I said no. I couldn't cope with being in a place where there were lots of people who I might have to talk to and listen to. Even thinking about it gave me anxiety. I was happy where I was, just me and Rip shooting the breeze.

But Rob wasn't taking no for an answer and kept nagging me. He said…

"Come on, mun Carl, it'll be a laugh, and you need to get out of this place. It's depressing in here, mun; it's no good for you being cooped up in this house all the time. It's not a nightclub or anything like that; it's an all-night party on a farm in the middle of nowhere."

"No, I'm alright, honest. You go, boys. Call back tomorrow and let me know how it went."

"What do you reckon, Simon? Do you think he needs to get out of this house as well?"

"I think we should respect his wishes, and if he doesn't want to come, then that's up to him. But we need to get a move on either way."

Rob grabbed the keys to the van out of Simon's hand, sat down next to me and said…

"We're not leaving unless you come with us. Simple as that. You can't stay in this house all the time, Carl, it's no good for you; it's like being in solitary confinement, and I know how that can fuck someone's head up, believe me."

"Don't worry about me, mun. Platoon is on later, and I got plenty of dope, and someone will probably call in for a chat. I won't be on my own all night."

"Carl, it's unhealthy. You have got to get out of your comfort zone and socialise with other people. We are not going anywhere unless you come with us."

I could see Simon looking at me as if to say, "For fuck sake, Carl, come on."

Rob grabbed the empty cups on the table…

"Who wants a cup of tea then, boys? Let's settle in for the night, shall we?"

Simon piped up, "Carl, just come out this once. If you don't like it, then you don't have to ever do it again. But don't spoil it for me; I really want to go to this party. My cousin reckons it's going to be wicked. They are all smokers so there won't be any trouble there."

"Okay. Fuck it. I'll never hear the end of it if I don't."

Rob looked over at me with a big smile on his face.

"Believe me, Carl, you will thank me for it later."

I put some food down for Rip and left the back door open for him to come and go. And off we all went.

The party on the farm turned out to be our very first rave. It wasn't an illegal rave but it was a rave. We left around eight o'clock. Simon had rough directions to the place from his cousin who lived down that area. It was only about half an hour away but we got lost trying to find it, so it took us just over an hour and in the end, we found it by accident. We noticed a load of cars parked up on the side of the road and people walking, so we parked up and followed them for about a mile through the lanes. We checked that they were going to the party and we weren't just following random people.

Eventually, we came to our destination; a rugged old farmhouse in the middle of nowhere. We met up with Simon's cousin outside; he asked us if we wanted any acid. Now, up until that time, I had only ever smoked dope and taken magic mushrooms. Although, when I was younger I sniffed Tipex thinner, hair spray, petrol, lighter fluid, glue, gas, and fire extinguisher (the small green ones found on a bus); not all at the same time, mind. The first time I sniffed glue, I was about nine years old. At the time, there were a lot of glue sniffers where I lived in Cardiff. I didn't really know what a glue sniffer was but

I had heard the word being said by my teachers and other older people. Then, one night, when my parents were out, three girls knocked on my door for my older sister. I answered the door and they stood in front of me, sniffing out of clear plastic bags. After they left with my sister, I noticed one of them threw their plastic bag on the floor so I went outside, picked it up, and started doing what they were doing with it, sucking in and out. It made the world go all funny and blurry, and I didn't know who I was or what my name was for a little while, but there was something about that feeling I did like.

Anyway, we all bought some acid from him; they were called "Strawberry Blotters." He told us they were a nice, light, giggly trip. They were £5 each. They looked like tiny stamps but instead of the Queen's head printed on them, there was a picture of a strawberry. The blotter bit was because they were on blotting paper. We all took them straight away.

There was music coming from inside the house. I'd never heard that type of sound before; lots of bass, bleeps, and industrial sounds. It was very raw and direct. I liked it. It reminded me a bit of Jean-Michel Jarre but much more urban and less synthesised. We all walked into the house; it was huge. It looked more like a big barn inside and there were people dancing all around, but the main concentration was in the living room area where the DJ was. I had never seen people dancing the way they were; it looked like they were doing some sort of Indian tribal dance, like a rain dance or something, and they were all in tune with the music. There were about two hundred people inside the house scattered about in different rooms. I started to feel a bit uncomfortable around so many people. I asked Rob and Simon if they wanted to go outside for a walk but they both said no. They wanted to be in the thick of all the action, so I went for a little walk on my own. There were a few people outside smoking dope and sitting about.

There was a small gazebo in the field behind the farmhouse; nobody was in there. I spotted a few of those white patio chairs underneath so I thought I'd go and sit up there on my own while I came up, but just as I was making my way towards it, someone grabbed hold of my hand. I looked 'round at a hippie-looking type of woman with long, wavy red hair, wearing a purple tie-dyed dress. I noticed she didn't have any shoes on.

"Come for a walk with me," she said.

I didn't have any choice; she was leading the way. We got inside the gazebo and she told me to sit down. I was about to pull up a chair but she said to sit on the grass. It wasn't wet, thank fuck, but even if it was, I don't think that would have mattered to her; I did as she told me and sat down. I wasn't sure what was going on. I was coming up off my trip as well. She sat down next to me and said...

"I can guess what star sign you are."

"Go on then."

"Sagittarius. You are the Archer, the fire sign. It means that your spirit is fuelled by passion and creativity."

"Yes, I am Sagittarius. What is your star sign?"

"I'm Aries, the Ram. It's also a fire sign like Sagittarius."

"What is your spirit fuelled by?"

"The pursuit of personal fulfilment."

I didn't know what to say to that so we sat in silence for a while, looking up at the stars. Then I asked her what her name was.

"Names don't matter here."

"Well, what shall I call you then?"

"You don't need to call me anything, or you can call me whatever you want. It's up to you."

"I'm going to call you Strawberry because you've got red hair and I just took a strawberry blotter. In fact, I'm going to give you two names; Miss Strawberry Blotter.

We both laughed at that and burst into a giggling fit. The acid was definitely kicking in. It was a nice, light, giggly trip, indeed.

When we stopped laughing, she looked me straight in the eye and I held her gaze for ages. She had freckles on her forehead and they looked like they were dancing with each other. Her eyes were bright blue and sparkly. I saw two little fairies flying around in them; they looked like Tinker Bell from Peter Pan. Then all of a sudden, they flew out of her eyes and landed on her nose. Then they whispered to each other, looked at me, giggled, and disappeared in a puff of wispy smoke.

It felt a bit weird just looking at each other, so I asked her…

"What else can you tell me about me?"

"I can tell that you are suffering from grief. You have good energy but you are not letting it out, and you won't allow anybody in to help you."

It was at that moment I burst into tears, but I wasn't feeling sad. I felt a sense of relief; the more I cried, the better it felt. So I kept on crying. I apologised to her, but she told me it was okay and to let it all out. She asked me to stand up. I did as I was told. When we both got to our feet, she hugged me, and I cried even more, but it felt good. I had heard of tears of joy before but never experienced them until then.

I don't know how long that lasted, but eventually, she said...

"It's time for you to talk about it now. It's time for you to say the words out loud and let them go."

We sat back down and I just opened up to her and told all the things that I had nobody else to tell, or didn't think I could tell, or didn't want to tell, and the more I was saying to her, the better I was feeling; it was weird as fuck. In my head, it felt like I was poking holes into a massive black sheet that was hanging over me and every new hole I made was letting in a bit more light each time. The more I was saying, the more holes I was making, and the lighter it was getting, and then when there was no more darkness to poke holes into. I stopped talking. We sat in silence for a while, and then Strawberry said...

"I'm going to leave you now, and you will never see me again."

"Where are you going?"

"I'm going where I have been."

"Where have you been?"

"That remains to be seen."

Then she hugged me, said goodbye, and ran off like Cinderella at midnight. And that was the last time I ever saw Strawberry Blotter.

Anyway, I'm not sure how long we were in the field but it felt like hours. I tried to work out what just went on but I couldn't make sense of any of it. I didn't even know if it was real. I looked around the field towards the house but couldn't see Strawberry anywhere.

But I did know that the darkness I'd been carrying around in my head was gone. I know I was tripping but I felt ten stone lighter, and I was only nine stone. Something had changed within me. I was no longer feeling anxious or paranoid about things. I wanted to mingle with the people in the house.

I spotted Rob and Simon in the living room amongst the crowd of people dancing, and I joined them. I had never really danced before except in discos when I was a kid. The music hit me in a different way than any other music had ever done before; it took me on a journey. I felt a connection to the music that I didn't even know existed. Everyone was dancing their own way and doing their own thing, yet, somehow, we were all connected. We were one machine, like pistons in a car, all working to make the engine run smoothly. At one point, as I was dancing, a shift in energy occurred; it felt like I had danced my way into another realm and inside that realm, each of us had a part to play.

Imagine a grandfather clock with a pendulum that swings back and forth. Now imagine the clock has stopped and needs winding up to start the pendulum swinging again. So now, think of the grandfather clock as the rave and the winding-up process as the music and the ravers are the mechanics behind the clock to keep the pendulum swinging, and we all have to work together in synchronicity to make sure that the clock keeps perfect time and the pendulum keeps swinging. That's what it felt like. I'm not sure if I am explaining it correctly but what I'm saying, in a very roundabout way, is when I started dancing that night, I was just dancing and joining in, but then, I wasn't just dancing. I became part of the mechanics of the clock. There was an unspoken under-standing amongst us, a shared sense that we were part of something bigger, something that was far more than just the farmhouse and the fields surrounding us. We were connected in ways we couldn't put into words but we demonstrated it through our movements, expressions, and unity.

I had never seen or experienced anything like that in my life, and I fucking loved it. I danced like nobody was watching. I didn't have a care in the world. None of us did.

When I took a break from dancing, I spoke to so many people, all in the same state as me. We'd burst out giggling at the sound of a word or a look on our faces, and even the simplest conversations were monumental. We had profound wisdom, insight, and clarity about everything and anything. We noticed connections between things that we had never seen before; there was a sense of honour and respect among us, and we were a family sharing the love. I spoke to Rob and Simon a few times. I told them all about Strawberry, so we all went on a mission to find her, but she was nowhere to be seen. Rob had bought another acid and was speaking in riddles but we understood what he was saying. Simon couldn't stop giggling; he was pointing at everything and bursting into laughter, describing what he saw in great detail. We couldn't see what he was seeing but he explained it perfectly enough for us to imagine it, and when the picture formed in our heads, we burst out laughing as well.

Anyway, the morning arrived as mornings always do; the sun came up, and we all came down, apart from Rob. The music stopped, and people started dispersing. I went outside to see if I could find Strawberry but I couldn't see her anywhere. I described her to a few people but nobody had even seen her at the party, and it wasn't as if she was easy to miss either, with her long red hair and sparkling blue eyes. I started to wonder if she was just part of my trip and if she ever existed at all. I even checked the area where we were sitting to see if the grass was flatter than the other bits of grass, but I couldn't tell. I wandered around the rest of the farm but she was nowhere to be seen. I wanted to tell her about my experience but mostly, I wanted to thank her for listening to me, helping me with my darkness, showing me the light, and being my spirit guide.

Just before we left, I noticed the DJ packing up. I asked him if he had any tapes I could have. I explained that I'd never heard anything like it before and didn't think I could buy it in Woolworths or HMV. He handed me a tape. The label on the tape read...

"Anasthasia T99 mix."

I put the tape on as soon as we all jumped in the van. The first sound from the tape was a crowd of people shouting, and then a woman's voice said...

Music Maestro, Please.

I did end up thanking Rob later because that conversation in my house changed everything for me. I'll always be grateful for what he saw happening to me and for having the insight to know exactly what needed to be done.

My Awakening

I woke up the next morning at two o'clock in the afternoon. It was a beautiful day outside. The sun was shining, and the swifts and the swallows were swooping through the streets, squeaking away. Rip was already up; he looked different. He had a grin on his face and swagger in his walk as he greeted me. I told him all about my night and what happened with Strawberry; he wagged his tail all the way through my tale. Whatever I was feeling and experiencing, he was feeling it too; I could tell by the look on his face. I made us both breakfast and opened the front door to let some fresh air in the house.

I sat down with a cup of tea and wrote this poem:

For a long time

For a long time I was lost, deep within myself.

For a long time I was lost, with nobody around to help.

For a long time I was alone, sitting on my own.

For a long time the lights were on, but nobody was at home.

For a long time I didn't understand and never knew why.

For a long time I smiled when all I wanted to do was
cry.

For a long time that was me, but not anymore.

Because now I know the fucking score.

I put the tape I had from the DJ on to make some copies for the boys. The first track that came on this time was…

Lennie De Ice – We Are IE

We are eeeee

We are eeeee

We are eeeee

I started dancing around the living room. I turned the volume up full-blast and got lost in it all over again. Then I started dancing in my hallway. My neighbours opposite were on their doorstep looking straight into my house, looking at me dancing. And then I danced on my doorstep, and a few people in the street watched me. Then I danced on the pavement outside and the people waiting outside the shop watched me. I didn't care; I was on my own, in my own world, but I wanted to show everyone that this was me. This was who I am. If you are happy and you know it, move your feet and dance in the street.

I found myself again and I was so relieved that I was still there. I was looking forward to finding out more about me and the rave scene. I danced for about three hours in the street on my own, in full view of all my neighbours and anybody passing by, only stopping to turn the tape over.

From that day onwards, I was reborn. As I said earlier, I have Rob to thank for that because he could see something I couldn't and he knew it was no good for me. I even started to wonder if he was Strawberry Blotter all along.

Got to Have House Music

About two weeks after that rave, Simon's uncle asked him to look after his house in Carmarthen for a week while he went on holiday. He invited me, Rob and Rip to spend the week down there with him, and since we weren't working and had fuck all else to do, we agreed. So on a Sunday night, we all went down to Carmarthen in Simon's van.

The house was about two miles from town, down a winding lane overgrown with bushes. His uncle was an old hippy, a bit of a recluse, but cool as fuck. He said we could have a party down there as long as we left the place as he left it. Luckily, he wasn't one of those clean freaks or anything like that. The house wasn't dirty but cluttered and a bit worn and tattered, the type of place you could wear your muddy work boots into the kitchen. He probably wouldn't notice if we organised a big fuck-off rave down there. It had five bedrooms, so we all had a room each. The outside was battered by years of wind and rain. There was moss creeping up between the cracks in the walls. The good thing about it, though, was that it had a big fuck-off barn outside and it was surrounded by fields. I knew Rip would like that straight away, and we all agreed it would be a good place for a rave.

Simon's uncle had left him money to buy food so on Monday, Simon and Rob went food shopping while me and Rip went for a walk to explore our surroundings. There was a river at the bottom of one of the fields and I found a good place to chuck Rip in. We decided to have the party on the Saturday night to give us plenty of time to organise it. Simon made a few phone calls to his cousins down that way and the arrangements were being undertaken. So for the rest of the week we chilled out, got stoned, and ate all the food. Rob made a big fuck-off bong out of a vase, some empty aerosol tubes, and a hose pipe. It was a beast, fair play to him; it looked like one of those Turkish water pipes. Some of Simon's mates would call up and we'd get stoned. The first thing Rob would do when he woke up was have a bong and a cup of tea, and the last thing he would do before he went to bed was have a bong and a cup of tea.

One morning, we woke up before him and filled the bong socket with bits of potpourri instead of a mix; we went into his room to wake him up with a cup of tea and his bong. He said...

"Fucking hell, boys, what's this? It's not my birthday."

"Thought we'd wake you up with a nice surprise."

"Well, I'm awake and I'm fucking surprised. So job done, boys."

I passed him the bong; he reached for his clipper lighter that he always kept at the side of his bed and held the top of the bong firmly to his lips to make sure no air escaped. He lit the socket and took a big fuck-off suck of it. And then he coughed and coughed some more and coughed again and again. We laughed our heads off.

He screamed at us…

"You fucking twats, what the fuck was that?"

"Potpourri."

"Are you fucking serious? Was there any mix in it or just all potpourri?"

"Just all potpourri."

We were pissing ourselves laughing and he was still coughing.

"That's not funny, boys; you don't know what's in that shit. It's from China; there could be all sorts of chemicals in it."

"It's okay, mun, it won't kill you; you can eat it and nothing will happen. You might not enjoy shitting it out but it's not poisonous."

"No, boys, that's not funny; that wasn't a nice experience. I take it all back now; it was a surprise but not a nice fucking surprise at all. You twats."

He was always apprehensive after that and wouldn't let anyone pack his bong for him. I don't blame him, mind; it was funny as fuck to watch though.

Anyway, by Friday, all the arrangements were made for a little party. Simon's mate down the pub sorted it all out and told a few select punters; only about fifty or sixty people, nothing too big. He even managed to get a sound system and a DJ to play all night, and he said he could get us some trips. We made the house party-proof; luckily, there was a big door at the bottom of the stairs that we could lock so nobody could wander off upstairs. The main part of the party would be in the barn but the chill-out areas would be the house; there was a downstairs toilet for the girls as well.

When Saturday arrived, Simon's mate called up in the afternoon to set everything up. He told us that a friend of a friend would bring our trips up later. We felt a bit apprehensive about the "friend of a friend" bit. We thought he might be bullshitting us, so we were a bit worried that our trips wouldn't materialise, but about an hour later, a guy called up on a motorbike with them. They weren't blotters though. He said they were "Purple Microdots"; we had never heard of any colour microdots, let alone purple ones. He held his hand out. It looked like he was holding little tiny bits of grain or dirt. Rob looked at them and said…

"What the fuck are they, mate? Are you taking the piss?"

"What do you mean? They're purple Microdots. Matt said you wanted some trips and here I am with trips for you. Fiver each. How many do you want?"

"They don't look fuck all like trips to me, mate. We wanted blotters."

"Oh boys, believe me, these are much better than blotters. Guaranteed, a twelve-hour trip."

"Listen, mate, you better not be ripping us off. We will come looking for you if you do."

"Well, you won't have to look far. I'm coming to your party tonight and dropping one myself."

We all bought one each from him and I wrote down the number plate of his bike.

At around six o'clock, Matt called up with the DJ and not long after that people started arriving, so we dropped our purple microdots. Rob remembered that he wanted a campfire later on in the field, so we both set off to collect some firewood while it was light and we were still capable. We left Simon to sort everything out. Rip stayed with Simon because he was enjoying the extra people fussing over him, especially the girls.

The rest of this story is kind of a bit fucked-up because one minute I remember me and Rob walking through the field looking for firewood; then the next thing I remember is us sniping around the field on our stomachs like the SAS. We even had branches sticking out of our clothes for camouflage and rubbed mud on our faces to blend in with our surroundings. We were taking cover behind some gorse bushes, lying in the thick of the grass, looking up at the house. The music was blasting, and people were dancing outside. Rob turned to me and said...

"Who the fuck are all them people? Where did they come from?"

"I don't know, there's loads of them. Did you invite them?"

"No, I didn't. Simon is not going to be happy at all; he'll go nuts when he sees all of them."

"Are you sure it's his uncle's house?"

"I think so; this field looks familiar."

"We need to rescue Rip."

"Yes, Rip is in danger."

"Yes, come on, but take your time. We got to watch out for snipers."

We started crawling slowly towards the house, making sure that no snipers in the windows spotted us. The next thing we knew, Simon was standing in front of us. He just appeared out of nowhere.

"Boys, these trips are fucking mental, the atmosphere in that house is crazy, I don't know what anyone is saying to me, I think they are all foreign… What are you doing on the floor?"

I looked up at him and said…

"We are going to rescue Rip."

The next thing I remember, I was in the kitchen and Rob and Simon were nowhere to be seen. Some guy came up to me with an empty soup bowl and a spoon, offering me a taste. he said…

"Have a taste of my magic soup."

"What's in it?"

"It's a secret recipe. Have some. Taste it, mmmm."

He scooped out an imaginary spoonful for me and I opened my mouth as if he were giving me some medicine. I liked the taste of it and asked him for more, but he said…

"You are only allowed one spoonful because it's really powerful, and there won't be enough to go around everyone. And I don't know how to make anymore because the evil witch stole the secret recipe from under my pillow."

"Is the evil witch in the house? Shall we go and find her?"

"No, I can't feel her presence, but she might come later."

Then he disappeared and in front of me was a girl holding Rip in her arms. She had wrapped him in a little pink blanket and he looked like a baby. He smiled at me and told me he loved me; I told him I loved him too. The next thing I knew, Rob came running up to me and said…

"Simon is having a downer."

"Why? What's he doing?"

He's sitting in the living room, blowing into a paper bag; he says he can't breathe. He's bringing other people down as well."

"He needs some magic soup. Come on, let's go and find the magic soup man."

As soon as I said, "Magic soup man," he appeared in front of us with his magic soup. We went to find Simon and he gave him a spoonful. It seemed to perk him up a bit and he stopped blowing into his paper bag. We all went outside for some fresh air. The DJ was playing…

Liquid – Sweet Harmony.

The next thing I remember; we were all in the barn dancing. Everyone was loving it. There was a good, happy vibe going on. There were about 100 people altogether, give or take a few. And then I was back in the living room with Simon. He was blowing into a brown paper bag, telling me he couldn't breathe. I called out for the magic soup man but he didn't appear. Simon looked at me, pointed to his mouth, and said...

"I can't breathe; all these people are stealing my air."

"There's plenty of air for everyone; don't worry, it's okay."

"It's not okay. I don't like it; I want everyone to leave."

"Stay by here; I'll go and find Rob. He'll sort you out, and he can bring some fresh air with him."

I went to look for Rob but couldn't find him anywhere. When I got back to the living room, Simon was sitting on Rob's lap, still breathing into a brown paper bag; Rob was rubbing his back. He looked at me and said...

"I think he's got colic. He can't breathe. I've managed to stop him crying."

Simon looked up at me and said...

"I want everybody to leave. I want you to tell them they all have to go home to bed."

He was pale and sweating like fuck, blowing in and out of the bag as if it was his lifeline; his face scared me a bit. He grabbed my arm and said…

"I can't breathe. I'm running out of oxygen. We need to evacuate everyone because they are stealing all the air from me, and you as well. They are taking it all, boys, and we have to get rid of them."

Rob looked at me and said…

"Carl. Tell them all to go. You have to. Tell them there is a fire or something."

So that's what I did. I went around to everyone and told them there was a fire and that they all had to leave. The next thing I knew, everyone was packing up, even the DJ. And then Simon calmed down, stopped breathing into the paper bag and said…

"It's okay now, they can all come back."

So I called them back and told them it was a false alarm. The DJ had already packed up and said he wouldn't unload his van again but that was okay; we told people we would light a campfire and sit around it and get a ghetto blaster to play music, so a few people came back. But then Simon started panicking again and told me to tell them all to leave, so that's what I did. We stood outside and watched them all go. When it was just the three of us left, we all started singing, dancing, and cele-brating that they had all gone. Simon was happy again. We could hear someone laughing from behind us. We turned around to see who it was, and it was the guy we bought the trips from. He said…

"See, I told you those trips were fucking wicked."

We all laughed, and Simon said he could stay because he was skinny and wouldn't take too much air. We some-how managed to light the campfire; it was a hell of a mis-sion though. We sat around it for the rest of the night and we all came down by about six o'clock in the morning. They really were twelve-hour trips… and what a fucking trip it was.

Our First Illegal Rave

It was the evening of Saturday, 20th July 1991. The Heineken beer festival was in Singleton Park in Swansea. Dr Feelgood was the headliner so it was busy. But we weren't there for the beer festival or Dr Feelgood. We weren't even inside the beer festival; we were in the car park because, according to Rob, someone had told him it was the meeting point for an illegal rave in Swansea that night. I did think it was an odd place to meet because ravers didn't drink alcohol or like being around pissheads, especially thousands of hardcore pissheads. Simon drove around the car park looking for ravers while me and Rob proceeded on foot.

We asked random people if they knew where the rave was but no fucker knew what we were on about; they didn't even know what a rave was. An hour passed and none of us had met any ravers or were any closer to knowing when or where it was. For all we knew, they could have met up already, or there wasn't even a rave at all and Rob had been given duff information. But then I spotted the DJ from the first party we went to walking out of the gates. I asked him if he knew about any rave that was supposed to happen and, as luck would have it, he knew all about it. He even handed me a little piece of paper with directions and where the meeting point was. As it turned out, it wasn't in the beer festival car park at all; it was in the car park of Toys R Us but that was only about a mile away. More importantly, we hadn't missed it. So Rob's source was a little bit unreliable but not totally. There was a rave but we were in the wrong place at the wrong time which, for once, worked out well for us.

Sure enough, when we got to the car park, about 20 cars and vans were already waiting. We chatted with a few ravers and bought some purple Ohms from one of them. They were blotters but a different kind of trip from a strawberry blotter. It was a deeper trip, more intense and thought-provoking. You would still get the giggles but there was more emphasis on exploring the depths of your mind, body, and soul with a purple Ohm trip. They didn't last as long as a purple microdot though, and weren't as mind-bending either.

The rave was in Kilvey Hill, about three miles away. None of us had heard of it before but apparently, it was a landmark in Swansea. Someone told us it was six hundred and thirty-three feet high; I had no conception of how high that was. I remember that bit vividly because I thought it was a shame it wasn't six hundred and sixty-six feet high.

Anyway, ten o'clock came and someone shouted to follow the red car. We did as we were told and followed the red car. Well, we followed a blue Ford Transit van, and he was following a yellow Mini, but somewhere along the line, someone was following a red car, and we were in our first rave convoy. It was exciting as fuck. We were part of an underground movement, escaping whatever bullshit life was throwing at us and building our own sub-community of Peace, Love, Unity, and Respect. It felt like something that happened in the Sixties. I have always said that the 90s were the 60s upside down. We needed our own form of escapism for our generation; something that belonged to us, something we could call our own, and we fucking found it.

We ended up driving through fields. It was uphill all the way; it was definitely high up, that's for sure. We passed cars and vans that people had ditched, deciding to walk the rest of the way. Simon was enjoying the challenge; he was used to driving on dirt tracks with his job. He managed to get us into the makeshift car park, which was just another field where lots of people seemed to have stopped. The rave was in the field next to it. We got out of the van, dropped our trips, and off we went.

As we walked towards the rave, I could hear that music again. It had the same beats, breaks and bleeps as we had heard at the last party. I had butterflies in my stomach, I felt like I wanted a poo but I couldn't see any toilets. There was a big camouflage marquee where the DJ was; a few people were dancing inside it and there were some people dancing in the field. We decided to split up, explore, and come up on our own. I noticed two girls dancing outside the marquee. One of them had a bright red jumpsuit on; it stuck out in a field full of green.

They looked cheerful as fuck, so I walked up to them to say hello, and they both hugged me; I wasn't expecting that. Then the girl in the red jumpsuit said...

"What's your name?"

"Carlos"

"Where are you from?"

"Neath."

"What have you done?"

"What do you mean what have I done?"

They both laughed at my answer.

"I mean, what have you taken tonight?"

"Oh right, yes, um… a purple Ohm."

It was the first time I had heard those three ubiquitous questions and the first time I had answered them. If you're a former raver yourself, you'll know those three questions were the standard greeting whenever you met anyone. I asked and answered them so many times after that night. Sometimes people ask, "What have you done?" or "What have you taken?" That was the most important of the three questions, the reason being you wanted to know if you had taken the same drug or drugs because if you had, you would be feeling the same buzz as they were feeling, and you could compare notes on the come up or whatever else was happening to you.

Anyway, I asked her what her name was, she told me, but I can't remember what it was, and then I said…

"Where are you from?

"Tenby"

"What have you done?"

"A double dove."

"What's a double dove?"

"It's ecstasy."

And then they both skipped off into the marquee. I made a mental note that the next rave I went to, I was going to try some ecstasy; a double dove, if I could get my hands on one, because I wanted to be as happy as they looked and felt.

About half an hour later, I could feel myself coming up off my trip. I always knew when I started tripping because the world felt wobbly and I felt wobbly, and all the colours around me would come alive and dance with each other. It was as if a veil had been lifted. You know that song, "I can see clearly now the rain has gone"? It was a bit like that, but "I can see clearly now my brain has gone" type of thing. I looked around for the boys. I spotted Rob and Simon at the bottom of the field down a slope next to a big electric pylon; someone was shouting at them to move away from it. I rolled down the slope on my stomach and landed at Rob's feet.

He didn't recognise me for a while, and then he said…

"It's you, mun Carl; I thought you were Simon."

"Simon is standing next to you, Rob. Look, he's over there." I pointed at Simon.

He stared at Simon for a while then turned to me and said…

"He told me he wasn't Simon but I knew he was Simon, but when I saw you, I thought you were Simon, and he was Simon as well, and everyone else here is Simon, and we all have to do what Simon does or Simon says."

I looked over to Simon…

"Well, what do you say, Simon?"

"It's simple," Simon said.

"What do you mean simple, Simon?"

"Wave to the pie man, wave to the pie man, wave to simple Simon," Simon said.

We all waved to the pie man, who was really Simon.

Well, that wasn't the exact conversation we had, word for word or any of them words at all. But it went something like that. You know the score.

There were about 200 of us in that field. The DJ was playing "Cola Boy – 7 Ways to Love." There was a very chilled-out atmosphere. People were cheerful, happy, and odd. Some danced in groups and others did their own thing. Everyone was smiling. I spoke to a few people and asked them the three ubiquitous questions. I can't remember their answers but mine were always the same: Carlos, Neath, Purple Ohm. It felt like we had all been friends for years. It was like being back in the school playground; like playtime in primary school. Some people were running around the field, chasing each other and playing off-ground touch. I even had a wheelbarrow race and a three-legged race; we used our socks to tie our ankles together. We rolled down the slopes on our stomachs and laid together on the grass, giggling at the bottom. There was a guy running around who thought he was a helicopter. We helped him to land, then he gave us all a ride in his helicopter and a tour of Kilvey Hill from above.

I'm not sure what time it was but the DJ dropped a track that stopped us all in our tracks. It was as if the

school bell had rung and it was time for assembly, or to
assemble. That track was…

"Zero B – Lock Up."

The intro came on and by the time the first beat
kicked in, we were all assembled on the dance field,
ready to stomp. We were under starters' orders, and then
we fucking stomped.

The next track he mixed in was…

"Joey Beltram – Energy Flash."

Baro, bo, bo, bo. Baro, bo, bo, bo.
Bo, bo, bo, bo. Baro, bo, bo, bo. Ba, ba, ba, ba.

Slowly, one by one, the music took us and drew us
in. We began to synchronise with each other. We all had
our unique and quirky way of dancing and expressing
how the music made us feel. After a few more tracks, we
were all connected, and we danced in unison non-stop for
the next five hours. We became part of the clock's mechanics and kept that pendulum swinging.

At some point in the early hours of the morning,
when it started to get a bit light, the police turned up.

They didn't come into the field; they just stood by the fence and watched us. There were only about five of them and I noticed some laughing at us. The first thing I thought of was "the laughing policeman". I don't think they knew what to make of it. In fact, I think it was their first illegal rave as well.

When the music finally stopped and it was time to leave, another adventure began; attempting to get out of the car park. All the cars were stuck in the mud so we were all giving each other a push. One guy even told me he had forgotten how to drive, so he was going to walk home and come back up when he remembered. Even the police were helping to push the cars. They could see everyone was off their face but they just wanted us off their patch.

All in all, it was a fucking brilliant night. It went quick, but it also went slow. We met a lot of people and made some good contacts in the rave scene. We felt we were part of them; they made us welcome and liked us all. That rave happened to be called *The Meaning of Life*, which I thought was very apt and on point because, up there in them there hills, we didn't have a care in the world. We were free spirits, united as one, just loving the moment we were living in; that, for me, was the meaning of life. We went to a few more *Meaning of Life* raves after that; they all had the same vibe and characters.

Our First Big Proper Rave

We had been handed a flyer for a big legal outdoor rave in Cambridge. It was called "Raindance – an Indian Summer" and was on a Saturday night. A reliable source told us they were the best events to go to if we wanted to experience a proper big rave, and that is precisely what we wanted to do. It was a good line-up as well:

Shades of Rhythm

Slipmatt

Guru Josh

Dave Angel

Urban Hype

There were plenty of other attractions to keep us amused: a free funfair, face painting, and ride simulators. There was even a postal service. I'm not sure why they had a postal service but you never know when someone might need to post a letter urgently. All sorts of weird and wonderful things happened in raves. It wouldn't surprise me to see a postman off his chops on the bouncy castle at three o'clock in the morning, flicking elastic bands at people.

We sorted out all the logistics back in my house. Simon could get a van from work and fill it full of red diesel, which saved us money on fuel costs. Tickets were on sale in Derrick's music shop in Swansea. Rob didn't want to spend money on tickets and said he would climb over the fence; he was old school like that.

Cambridge was about 250 miles from where we lived. It would take us roughly four hours to get there so, after much deliberation and debate, we decided we might as well make a weekend of it and travel up on the Friday afternoon. That way, we could find where the rave was, sleep in the van close to it, and maybe even bump into some other ravers and score some double doves. We all wanted to try them out. We had heard so many good things about them from other ravers; not just double doves but ecstasy in general, or MDMA, as they say. We were even told that in some countries, they give people ecstasy in therapy sessions because it's good for dealing with PTSD; it helps people to open up about things and show their emotions.

Anyway, Friday arrived; we were meant to leave at around ten o'clock, but Simon had an emergency thing going on with his girlfriend that lasted all fucking day, so eventually we left a five o'clock. But before we left, Rob insisted on putting his double mattress in the back of the van because he wanted it nice and cosy if we were going to sleep in it; he even brought his cushions and a quilt. It did look cosy as fuck as well, so we all grabbed our quilts and it looked like one of those Harem tents. Rob wanted to bring his bedside cabinet and a lamp as well, just for a laugh, to make it look like an actual bedroom, but we talked him out of that. He did have a rule that we all had to take our shoes off, though, which was fair enough; it was his bed, after all.

We had a new tape to play on the way up: Easy Groove in Perception – The Summer Celebration in Long Marston Airfield. I had ordered it from a number on the back of a flyer and, as luck would have it, it arrived on Friday morning. None of us were allowed to listen to it until we started our journey, then we put it on full blast as standard; it was a good tape, too. Easy Groove was like a God to us; none of us had been to a rave where he had played but that was next on our list. We were about five miles from Cambridge town on the B roads when the van started spluttering and jerking. Rob thought Simon was joking and shouted to him…

"Stop fucking about, will you? I'm trying to roll a joint."

"Rob, I'm not fucking about. Something's wrong; I'll have to pull over."

"Well, pull over fucking smoothly then. I don't want to tip this joint; I packed it."

We pulled over into a lay-by. The engine cut out before we stopped.

We had plenty of diesel and the gauge was showing the tank as half full. We looked on the road where we had come from but there was no trail of oil or any other liquid leading to us; it was starting to get dark as well. I looked at the time; it was nine-thirty. We were in the middle of nowhere; there were no other cars on the road and no road signs about to indicate where we were. We lifted the bonnet; none of us knew about engines but it seemed like the obvious thing to do. We didn't have a torch either, and there were no streetlights. We thought the engine might have overheated, or a rabbit might have got stuck in the fan belt or something. But the engine seemed to be at a normal temperature and no rabbits were rammed between anything. Simon tried turning the engine over a few times, but it wouldn't bite. We were fucked; well, *we* weren't but the van was. We had a little debate amongst ourselves about what to do next and decided that there was fuck all we could do about it; we might as well get stoned, sleep in the van for the night, and try to get it sorted in the morning. We all jumped into the back of the van, feeling so glad that Rob had brought his mattress; at least we would have a decent night's sleep.

We woke up at about ten o'clock. Rob opened the van doors to let some light and fresh air in; it was a lovely morning. We got out of the van and took in our surroundings. We had parked in a small lay-by, only enough for one vehicle. It was next to a field with bushes and hedges all around. Rob jumped onto the roof of the van to get a better view of where we were.

"Fucking hell, boys, we're here; the rave is in the next field. Come and look!"

We all jumped on the roof; it was good that we didn't have our shoes on.

"Easygroove, Easygroove, Easygroove." Rob shouted, "Reach for the sky, reach for the sky."

We had broken down right outside the car park to Raindance but on the other side of the entrance. We could see the marquee and the fun fair; they were still setting things up. We couldn't believe it, so we all rolled a celebratory joint and sat on the van, watching the workers set things up.

We decided that the first thing we needed to do was find out what was wrong with the van and get it fixed. After that? Fuck knows.

Simon tried starting the van up; the engine turned over, and it was purring like a pussy cat. We thought it must have just needed a rest. We all jumped in and he set off, but then it started spluttering and jerking again. We were moving, although not very fast; he managed to get it up to about 20 miles an hour. We spotted signs for the town and followed them while the traffic built up behind us. People honked their horns and waved their arms out of the windows at us. We just imagined that we were the lead vehicle in a rave convoy. We spotted a garage and Simon pulled into the forecourt. He went looking for a mechanic and returned with one a few minutes later. He started the van up, then looked under the bonnet, shook things about, untwisted things and moved a few pipes around. He looked at Simon and said...

"You know it's illegal to use red diesel on public roads, right?"

"Is there red diesel in there? Fucking hell, I told them to fill it up with white. I work on the roads and the boys take care of the vans.

"It's okay, I'm not the police but they do a lot of spot checks around this area, so you better be careful. Your filter is clogged up. It's full of shit from the red diesel that your mates put in, so it's going to need changing."

Rob piped in. "How long will that take, mate?"

"I'll have to order it in. It might be here on Monday or Tuesday at the latest.

"Aw, look, mate, is there any chance you can clean the filter out or something? You don't have to give it a good clean like, just enough for it to get us back to Wales."

"Where in Wales are you from?"

"Swansea." We all said at the same time.

"Fucking hell. Driving around with red diesel in the van and you got the DVLA on your doorstep. I'll see if I can get one of the boys to look at it; it won't be until this afternoon, mind."

"How much will it cost, mate?"

"Easy, tiger; I don't know if it can be fixed yet. Come back around four o'clock and if it's done, consider yourselves lucky. If it's not, well, you know the drill."

We left the van with him, walked into town, and found a café. We all ordered a full breakfast. The rave didn't start until nine o'clock so we had all day and a bit of the night to kill. We spent most of the day in Cambridge town. It was a quaint place with some beautiful buildings; a little bit Shakespearean. It looked like a place where lots of rich people and academics, like professors, archaeologists, and antique collectors, lived. We had a few stares from people because of how we were dressed in our full rave gear. We looked like some sort of children's TV presenters. When we returned to the garage around four o'clock, the van was ready for us, and so was the mechanic; he had cleaned the filter as best he could, drained all the red diesel out and put a fiver's worth of white in. He reckoned it should get us back to Wales but if it didn't, it would at least get us closer. Altogether, it came to £45. We divided the cost between us, even though Simon tried to argue that he shouldn't have to chip in for the diesel. Rob argued back that it was Simons' fault for putting red diesel in the van in the first place. But in the end, we all paid equal amounts and off we went.

We headed straight for the rave and luckily, the car park gates were open early. Some people were already there so we walked around the car park, chatting with people and looking to score. We didn't have to look far; there was a guy sitting in the back of a van with the doors wide open, shouting…

"E's, speed, acid, blow."

We approached with caution.

"Alright, boys? What are you after? What can the doctor get you?"

Simon whispered, "What E's have you got?"

"No need to whisper, mate. There's no police around unless you lot are undercover cops. I've got China Whites, Phase Fives and Double Doves."

"How much are the double doves?"

"£20 each boys"

"I'll have two double doves, please, Doctor." Rob chipped in.

They exchanged cash and pills. Me and Simon bought one each. Rob had always been a bit of a greedy bastard and wanted to make sure he was right off his chops. We decided we would drop our pills half an hour before the gate opened, so we mingled around the car park, meeting people while we waited. We met all sorts of oddballs and felt right at home. There was an offbeat atmosphere around the place; you could feel the anticipation in the air. Everyone was very excitable; not excited, but excitable. People danced and skipped around the field, weaving in and out of the cars.

I saw strangers shaking hands, saying, "How do you do?" A few hours later, they were hugging and saying, "I fuckin love you." I reckon Louis would have approved.

Anyway, at around about eight o'clock we all dropped our pills. Rob didn't have a ticket so he wandered off to look for a weak spot in the security, like a fence or a wall he could climb without being detected. As he was walking away, he shouted back to us...

"See you later, boys. It'll be easy to find me; I'll be in the hardcore tent dancing on the stage. Stomp, stomp, stomp it on."

Just after eight-thirty, they opened the gates and we all queued up. My guts were turning over at the expectation of what was about to come. The music coming out of the main tent reverberated around us. BOOM, BOOM, BOOM. None of us could keep still. Our legs were going, jaws were chomping, heads were nodding, and we all had big cheesy grins on our faces. When I got inside, the first thing I needed to do was have a poo; my stomach was in knots and I had to release the tension before it released itself of me. I went to the portaloos and Simon went to get his face painted. I sat on the toilet, took a deep breath, and let it all out. When I finished, I opened the door and could hear the DJ in the main tent playing...

Sound Corp – Dream Finder.

And I was up off my pill. It felt like I had just opened the door to Wonderland. The lights of the funfair were sparkling and every colour was exaggerated, almost cartoonish. I could see people jumping up and down on the bouncy castle. When they were in mid-air, it looked like they were in slow motion. My whole body was tingling, and waves of warmth radiated through me; everything had a glow around it, even the ground underneath me felt soft and bouncy, the beats of the music were pulsating through the floor and through my body, thumping in sync with my heartbeat; the sound of the bass was tingling through my spine. Someone tapped me on my shoulder; I turned around. I didn't know who it was but we hugged each other. Then he asked me...

What's your name?
Where you from?
What have you done?

I asked him the same three questions back. I can't remember his name or where he was from, but he had also taken a double dove. Like I said earlier, the thing about that third question being the most important is that you want to know if someone is on the same trip as you so you can compare notes on the come-up or the feelings you're experiencing. It was another way of bonding with someone. A few other people gathered around us and we all hugged each other, squeezing as tight as we could as we hugged and rushing with every squeeze. I felt like I was in the exact place that the universe wanted me to be and surrounded by people that I was meant to meet and be with. I was in love with the whole wide world.

I went on the waltzers a few times and met loads of people. I liked spinning around; it brought me up more and made me rush. I had a good laugh on the bouncy castle as well. It felt like we were all kids again in the playground; we were all having so much fun and none of us had a care in the world. I had never experienced an atmosphere like it. It felt like we were all in a circus and we were the performers. I sat down and chatted with random people and had some bizarre conversations, laughing, hugging, and rolling about the floor, feeling the grass; everyone was just so genuine and sincere. It was as if we'd stepped into a shared dream. Our frequencies were aligned and our vibrations were in tune with one another. It was pure euphoria.

I spent most of my time in the garage tent. The dance floor was empty when I first got in there but quite a few people were sitting around getting stoned; they were using it as a chill-out area. I sat with a few of them until Guru Josh came on and opened up with "Infinity". I went straight to the middle of the floor and started dancing; people began to join me. Not long after that, the place was packed, and I was commanding the dance floor and setting the vibe. It was beautiful. Guru Josh played a blinding set. As I walked out of the garage tent for some fresh air, someone passed me and said…

"Shades of Rhythm are coming on in the main tent."

And then I heard:

Here's another chance for you to dance with me.
Here's another chance for you to dance with me.
Here's another chance.
Here's another chance.

When I got inside, the first thing I noticed was Rob was on stage dancing with the Shades of Rhythm dancers; that brought me right up, and then I spotted Simon on a podium dancing with a load of other people, so I went to join him. The next track they played had the place fucking bouncing. It was…

Extacy.

Sky's the limit and you know you that can have what you want.

The whistle posse was out, horns were blowing, hands were in the air. We were in ecstasy. The sky was the limit, and we knew.

We all met up in the car park in the morning when it was kicking out time. Rob was still off his face; he hadn't long dropped his other dove and he was loved up to fuck. He'd managed to sneak in over a fence but landed waist-deep in the stingy nettles. His arms were scratched to fuck but he didn't care; he couldn't feel any pain. It was mad that we didn't see each other most of the night but we liked that and decided that every rave we went to, we would split up as soon as we got through the gates and do our own exploring and meeting people; that way we wouldn't have to rely on each other and if we happen to bump into each other then so be it, but if we didn't then so be it as well.

We had a good laugh in the car park, staying there for hours; it added another element to the rave. I caught up with loads of people that I had seen throughout the night and we hugged again, said goodbye, and told each other to take care.

So, all in all, our first big rave was a massive success, and the double doves lived up to our expectations. You don't need wings to fly.

Pulse – Swansea University

We had been told that there were rave nights being held at Swansea University called "Pulse." It was run by the *Tick Tock* Crew (not the TikTok we know today), who were from Swansea. They also had some rave nights in the infamous "Dirty Dora's" nightclub in Swansea and Martha's nightclub, which I will tell you about later. They were known for throwing the best parties, legal and illegal, so we figured we needed to head down there and get in amongst it all. So that is exactly what we did one Saturday night. We didn't know who was playing down there so when we arrived at the car park and got talking to a few people, we were pleasantly surprised to hear that Utah Saints were the headliners. We loved a bit of Utah Saints. *U, U, U, Utah Saints.*

We didn't have a lot of money and what we did have, we wanted to keep for refreshments, so we needed to try and avoid paying to get in. Rob was going to try to sneak in anyway so we thought we'd join him. There were a few people down there with the same idea. It wasn't a lot of money to get in, but I think it was the thrill of the chase to see if we could get in without paying. Someone spotted a small window open in the toilets around the side; it was one of them top windows that opened out, and not very wide either. A medium-sized person would struggle but would manage to do it with a bit of wriggling and maybe someone pushing them, but a skinny fucker like me would fly through there. And that's how we all got into our first Pulse; it became a bit of a tradition to try to sneak in after that.

Anyway, Pulse was where we honed our raving skills and truly became part of the rave family. We got to know so many people and made some crazy-ass friends. It was proper hardcore in Pulse and everyone knew the score. It was total madness and mayhem from the minute you walked through the door or climbed through the window; everyone was off their face and steam was coming off people's clothes because they danced so much. Pulse was the place where you dressed to sweat. The temperature in there was like a tropical forest. It smelt of poppers and Vicks vapour rub. People would be wringing the sweat out of their T-shirts. I always remember one guy with a white "Raveon" T-shirt; it was a piss-take of "Radeon." The way he danced was inspiring, motivating, and con-tagious. He would get the crowd going, build them up, and take them to the skies.

We went to quite a few "Pulse" nights; in fact, it was where we got to see Easy Groove for the first time. Only once do I remember us having to pay to get in; the rest of the time, we sneaked in using various methods. There was one time we noticed that the stamp they were putting on people's hands for re-entry was fluorescent green, very much like what's inside a glow stick, and because the people who wanted to go outside were sweating, the stamp on their hands would distort and not resemble a stamp at all; it was more like a fluorescent blob. One of our friends who was inside came out and she happened to be wearing a glowstick bracelet. So we asked her if she wouldn't mind us tearing it apart and rubbing the fluorescent fluid on our hands. She happily obliged because that's what ravers would do for each other. It worked, too; it passed the fluorescent stamp detector test.

The only thing was that Pulse wasn't an all-nighter; we would have loved that. It finished at around two o'clock, and it was after one of the Pulse raves that we first experienced going to the services, which was another part of the whole scene. Every rave had its own story, with a beginning, a middle, and an end. The car park was the beginning, the rave was the middle, and the services were the end. It was in Pulse where I had my most memorable rave but not for the reasons you might be thinking of. Oh no, it was the complete opposite, and I will take you through it step by step because I remember it vividly:

It all started when I bought an E called a "splinter," which was a capsule. Apparently, there was MDMA, amphetamine, and acid in them. They weren't from up England, where the pills would typically come from; it was some guy in Swansea who was making them in his kitchen. It's a hell of a mix of chemicals, though. The MDMA made you all lovey, the speed made you bouncy, and the acid made you trippy.

Now, the thing about capsules that I didn't know at the time was that they take longer to get into your system than a tablet. Anyway, I took one and was waiting to come up off it, but after about half an hour, I wasn't feeling anything. Usually, by then, I would have felt some tingling or some little rushes, so I waited a little bit longer but still fuck all. I went looking for the guy I bought it from but couldn't find him so I decided to buy another one from someone else. About half an hour later, I came up off my pill and was on the dancefloor stomping away, in the thick of it all. The place was vibrating and pulsating with energy. If you could bottle that shit, you could sell it in a capsule for £20 a pop.

Utah Saints came on and dropped the track we were all waiting for...

What Can You Do for Me?

What can you do for me?
I need someone.
What can you do for me?
I need you I need you.
You wanted the best,
And you got the best.
Utah Saints.

They also dropped a brand new track that they hadn't released and we'd never heard:

Something Good.

Fuck me, the place went ballistic. It was a belter of a track, a proper anthem. It sampled Kate Bush's song "Cloudbusting" and her vocals. It set the theme and the buzz for the rest of the night. It was a fucking power-house of dance in there. I stomped as hard as I could in the same spot for about two hours. At one point, I remember Simon handing me a bottle of water and shouting in my ear.

"You need to drink some water."

So I drank some water. Then, sometime after, Rob was by my side, handing me water.

"Carl. Drink this and go and have a sit-down; you've been dancing in the same spot for hours."

"I can't. I love it, Rob; I couldn't stop dancing even if I wanted to"

He handed me the bottle.

"Just make sure you drink plenty of water."

The next thing I remember, I was falling into people and they were pushing me off them. People were moving away from me, and then I fell to the floor and blacked out.

I don't know how long I was out for but I remember people lifting me from the floor. As soon as they got me to my feet, I started trying to dance again but I was too wobbly and fell over. Eventually, they got me steady on my feet, took me outside, and sat me down for some fresh air. They gave me some water and told me to come back inside when I felt better. They all left but a girl I didn't know stayed with me to make sure I was alright. After about half an hour, I told her I felt better and was ready to go back inside. She told me that if I could walk up the steps without help, I could go back inside; I just about managed it, although I had to hold onto her a little bit. When we got inside, she insisted that I sit down for a little while, so she took me over to the side of the stage out of the way and told me to have a break, then I could dance again. I sat on the floor, watching everyone dance. I looked around and I couldn't work out where I was, what place I was in or who I was with. I could see people all around me. I knew they were people but didn't know what "people" were. I knew people were boys and girls, but I couldn't determine what a "boy" or a "girl" was. All I knew was that they were called "people", and I kept repeating the same phrase in my head over and over again…

What is a boy? What is a girl?
What is a boy? What is a girl?
What is a boy? What is a girl?

The more I said it, the further away the answer was getting from me. I couldn't take it anymore so I stood up and headed for the exit; I opened the doors, ran down the stairs, out of the building, down the steps, and then collapsed on the pavement and had a full-on fit. Like, an epileptic fit in front of everyone outside at the time, including the ice cream man parked in front of the building.

Now, what I'm about to say might seem corny as fuck but it's true, honest. I can't say my life flashed before my eyes but parts of my life certainly did, as I was on the floor having a fit. In my head, I thought I was lying in a field, but not in the middle of a field; I was near a gate and everyone was looking down at me. They were people that I knew from my life, like my brothers and sisters, people I was in school with or a shopkeeper. I didn't see my mother, though, but I saw my stepfather. It felt like that scene in The Wizard of Oz when the house flies away and spins up in the air, and people's faces appear. Nobody knew what to do with me; in fact, they gave me a wide berth. People who had come outside for some fresh air ran straight back through the doors as soon as they spotted me. That type of shit is frightening to witness when you are tripping and could put you into a right downer.

When I finally shook myself out of it (pun intended), I saw what I knew were two real people looking down at me: Simon and a paramedic. The paramedic helped me to sit up, shone a torch in my eyes, and asked me my full name. I gave him my full name. He looked to Simon to check that it really was my name. Simon gave him a nod of approval. He got up and chatted with Simon for a little while. I couldn't make out what they were saying. I could hear a boy screaming behind me…

"I'm going to kill him. Get him away from here or I'll kill him."

"I'm going to kill him now."

No doubt I was freaking him right out and he was having a downer because of me; he caught my downer. Anyway, Simon came back with a piece of paper in his hands and handed it to me. I couldn't read it but it was some sort of disclaimer he had to sign to say he would look after me, and there was nothing more the paramedics could do for me. He helped me to my feet and sat me out of harm's way against the front wall. I told him to go back inside because I was worried he might catch it too; he looked like he might be on the edge a bit and anything could tip him into it. He didn't ask me if I was sure. He took the opportunity and fucked off. I would have done the same.

I sat there for a while. My mind was completely blank and I felt nothing. My lips were bleeding and swollen because during my fit, I had clenched my top teeth against my bottom lip and bit so hard I could feel teeth marks. I was still up off my pill and was feeling stunned by what had happened. I was trying to make sense of everything, hoping I wouldn't have another fit or a downer.

"Have some of this, Carl. It will bring you down."

Someone was passing me a carton of orange juice. I looked up to see who it was; it was a boy I was in school with that I hadn't seen for years. I didn't even know he was into raves or had ever seen him in a rave. The straw was already in the carton and I sucked the whole thing dry until it made a squeaking noise. Then off my mate went.

Within about ten or fifteen minutes, I had come around and was thinking clearly and rationally, and I knew what a boy and a girl were. I knew where I was and the gravity of the situation I had put myself in. I figured that I'd had some sort of overdose. The first pill wasn't a dud; it was just taking longer to kick in. I probably came up on pill number two right about the time pill number one was reaching its peak potential, which is why I couldn't stop dancing. So, in the end, my body said...

"Fuck this for a game of soldiers. I'm taking him out and I'm going to shake him violently for a while."

I didn't want to go back inside. I felt embarrassed and ashamed. Loads of people saw me and knew what had happened to me, and I might spin them out, so I waited outside for it to finish. I sat there for about an hour. The girl who had helped me earlier on in the night sat with me for a while and I kept apologising to her, but she said there was no need and was glad I was back to normal. Simon came out with Rob and found me sitting in the same spot he had left me. Rob said people inside were telling him that I had a fit outside and on a downer but he said he didn't want to come and see me in case I put him into a downer, and he knew people were looking after me. I don't blame him for doing that at all. I wouldn't have liked him to see me in that state either.

We all still went to the service station afterwards but I sat outside because I didn't want to spin people out. That incident should have frightened the fuck out of me, and Rob and Simon. We all should have said no more raves after that. But that would have been the sensible thing to do. Admittedly, it messed my head up for a bit, made me a little paranoid, and took away some of my newfound confidence, but that didn't last long.

Patti Pavilion – Kinetic

Things were getting really busy in my house. The mood was bouncy and bright, even though the walls were still brown. I wasn't writing any more depressing poems; I was still writing stuff, but it was all upbeat and quirky:

The pattern on the wall
Once upon a time in a pattern on a wall
there grew a room the size of a hall
the pattern exploded and became a town.
The King who ruled it lost his crown
his wife, the Queen was very sad
she despised the pattern that made him mad
so she sent for a Knight to banish the pattern
but they fell in love and now live on Saturn.

When Rob and Simon called down, we would spend hours looking at flyers, working out what rave to go to next. So obviously, everyone else who came to my house wanted to go to a rave and immerse themselves in the experience like we were doing. They wanted to experience what we were explaining to them; they were eager as fuck for it. So we wrote a list of all the names of the people who were in our social circle. We had three categories:

1. Definitely.
2. Maybe.
3. Most definitely not.

We had people in mind that we thought would absolutely love it and live it. There were others we were worried wouldn't be suitable for the scene for various reasons; we thought some wouldn't be able to handle the drugs and the head that came with it, some wouldn't be able to handle the people and the head that came with them. Then there were the ones we thought the ravers wouldn't be able to handle; the boys who liked to get drunk, had a bit of an attitude after a few pints, and were likely to start a fight or pick on some fucker for looking odd or dancing weird or just talking to them. You know the type; we all knew or know someone like that. Eventually, after lots of deliberation, we got the list of names down to sixteen people. The next thing to work out was where to take them, and after lots more deliberation, we found the perfect place: a local rave called "Kinetic" in the Patti Pavilion Club in Swansea. It wasn't an all-nighter, it closed at two o'clock, so we thought it would be a good place to start them off, and it was close enough to home to jump in a taxi and get the fuck out of there if they didn't like it. Also, it was in the Christmas holidays on the 28th of December; no better time to take them to a proper fucking party. Celebrate good times, come on!

So everything was arranged with the chosen few. We gave them all a pep talk on what to do and what not to do in raves. We told them not to dress like they were going to a nightclub; dress to sweat and to wear something a bit colourful. Ravers were a bit wary of people who looked like they belonged in a nightclub because they were usually pissheads who would stand around in groups, holding their drinks and laughing at other people, then get funny if someone bumps into them. So they needed to blend in so they would be more approachable and not so hostile looking. We also gave the talk about the dangers of drugs and taking too much, not drinking enough water, having plenty of rest, and going to the chill-out room if they felt they were a bit too fucked. Another important thing we told them is that once we get inside, we split up, and they should split up too, and certainly not congregate in one area or walk around together everywhere like they do in the nightclubs. We told them to explore the place, talk to people, dance, and let the music take their bodies.

Anyway, twas three nights after Xmas 1991. Bohemian Rhapsody was the Christmas number one. Simon had sorted a van out from work and we were all in my house waiting for everyone to arrive. As expected, they all started turning up and all looked very colourful. They'd taken my word literally and some looked like they were going to a fancy dress party dressed as clowns. It was fucking brilliant. They would blend in *and* stand out, but in a good way, and might even get more attention from people than they expected; it was all part of the fun. We handpicked each and every one of them so we'd done the psychological profiling bit on them and knew they'd all be able to handle it. Well, we hoped they would anyway.

When the time arrived to leave, we all piled into the van. Getting sixteen rookie ravers in the back was a tight squeeze but Rob had put all his cushions from his three-piece suite in and I added mine too, so they all had something to sit on. It wasn't a long journey; half an hour at the most. The three of us sat in the front of the van and had plenty of room.

We had to queue outside for quite a while when we got down there. I remember it being freezing and a pay-at-the-door event, which also slowed the process down a bit. There were people outside selling the refreshments.

None of them had any ecstasy though, so we all bought some acid. I can't remember what ones they were but we all had the same. We told them to only buy one each at first and then, if they wanted more, they could buy some inside. Me and Simon bought two each and Rob bought four. Most of them had taken magic mushrooms before so they knew what it was like to trip. When we all got inside I left them to it, and off I fucked to play.

Now as for the rest of the night, I can't recall many details, but what I can remember, I'm happy to share. The atmosphere was exactly the same as all the other parties we had been to; hot, sweaty, and proper hardcore, with loads of brilliant dancers on the stage and the dance floor, getting the crowd going. I saw a lot of the people from Pulse so it was good to meet up again and form more dancing bonds with them, have a laugh, and talk absolute bollocks. One of the DJs playing was DJ Jamo from the Tick Tock Crew. He played a wicked a set and got the place bouncing.

I don't remember much more from that night, although I found some videos on YouTube and spotted me, Rob and Simon in them. It's the only footage I can find of us in a rave back in the early days. As for everyone we took to their first rave, some of them ended up walking around together all night, soaking it all in and enjoying themselves; others took to the dance floor like they had come out of the womb raving and are still hardcore ravers to this day. Two of them didn't have a good time at all and spent most of the night in the chill-out room feeling a bit frightened and overwhelmed; they never went to another rave again. We ended up going to the services as well, then back to my house in the morning to swap stories about all the fun and frolics we had.

Simon's Job Offer

Somewhere around February 1992, Simon was offered a job with a promise of shit loads of money, but he needed two people in his gang. Now normally, the last people he would have thought of asking were me and Rob because we were way too busy in the days doing fuck all to be working and getting up in the morning and having to leave the house and do work stuff. However, he did ask us and, of course, we politely declined his offer and laughed at the thought, until he told us a little bit more about what it entailed and how we could greatly benefit from it.

So there was this guy called Mick. He was an Irishman. Everyone called him "Mad Mick" because, by all accounts, he was a mad bastard. Legend had it that the police didn't ask Mick to help them with their enquiries; Mick asked the police to help him with his enquiries. Nudge nudge, wink wink, say no more. Mick had acquired a sizeable plot of land in Carmarthen with the aim of building a bunch of houses on it and selling them to a bunch of people with a bunch of money. Simon met him one night in a pub. They got chatting at the bar and Simon mentioned to Mick that he worked on the roads, making plans and organising gangs, the usual stuff that we told him not to talk about to us. But unlike us, Mick was very interested indeed because, as I mentioned earlier, he was building a little housing estate that needed roads and drainage and kerbs and pavements; all the usual stuff you find on every street. So, to cut a long paragraph short, after a few pints and lots more talk about kerb laying, tarmac, and drainage, Mick offered Simon the contract to do all the work. They negotiated a price, double the amount that Simon was earning, and the contract was signed. Well, they shook hands on it, had a few more pints, and discussed the finer details. Which Simon later relayed to us in my living room…

"It's a four-month contract, possibly extended to five, depending on circumstances. I need two people in my road gang; a dump truck driver and a labourer. Carl, you'll have to be the labourer because you can't drive."

"Wait a minute. I haven't even accepted your job offer yet, and you're not exactly selling it to me at the moment."

"What's the pay?" Rob asked.

"It's £250 a week cash in hand. But we'll all have to move down to Carmarthen until the contract ends."

"Where will we live? Will we have to pay for digs out of the 250?"

"No. This is the best bit, boys. We'll be staying in a six-berth luxury caravan on Mick's land. We'll all have a bedroom each. We don't have to pay any rent, and we get breakfast and dinner cooked for us every day. Well, five days a week."

"None of us eat on weekends anyway. Do we have to work weekends?"

"Not every weekend, but there will be some weekend work if we are rained off or if there are delays with materials."

"How come we get fed as well, then? Who will be feeding us?"

"His wife; she's from the Philippines. There's a lot of work going on down there. She runs the canteen and does all the cleaning."

"What? So he has bought a wife to work and now he wants to buy some kids? He Sounds dodgy as fuck to me."

"It's not like that, mun; he didn't buy her from the Philippines. His first wife ran off with another man, and she was the cleaner, so they got together. I've met her; she's lovely and a good cook as well."

"What will we have to do down there? As in, is it hard graft like?"

"No, I've sorted out a gang of boys from down that area. They'll do most of the roadworks, pathways, and kerb laying. You just both need to be on hand to help out."

"So, is there anybody else living down there as well?"

"There's another guy called Gus. He's the site manager. He's a bit of a pisshead but a good worker. He's in a caravan next to ours."

"I still don't get why we need to live down there."

"Well, travelling to Carmarthen every morning would be a nightmare. We'd have to get up at five o'clock because the roads are so busy. And I told him that you'd do a bit of security work on the site as well."

"What do you mean? Like security guards?"

"Sort of. He's having a bit of trouble with tools going missing and machinery being stolen in the night. So he just wants an extra presence down there to prevent it from happening."

"So he wants us to be bouncers as well?"

"We probably won't have to do fuck-all; just be on hand if there's any trouble or just take a walk around the site now and then in the nights."

"What do you reckon, Carl? We're going to have to do some work; that's the shit part. But think about it. We could use it as a base to go partying all over West Wales.

Fuck-all is happening up this way, it's all going on down there. That's where we should be; smack bang in the middle of it."

"And it also comes with a company Ford transit van and plenty of red diesel, boys." Simon chipped in chirpily.

Rob looked over at me and said...

"Carl. Imagine it. All of us are living together: me, you, and Simon. We'll be like students on campus."

"Can I take Rip?"

"I don't know, I'll have to ask Mick."

"Aw, Carl, I'd rather you didn't", Rob said pissed-offily.

"Why? What's wrong with taking Rip? He comes with my territory."

"Just leave him with your stepfather. I don't mind him in your house, but I don't want to live with him in a caravan. He's a towel shagger, mun. I've caught him doing it a few times. He did it in front of me once when I was sitting on the toilet having a shit."

"Well, he can't help it. He's fucking lonely."

"He's not fucking lonely, Carl, he's fucking towels. It's disgusting, mun. I don't want him down there with us. I might pick up a towel he has spunked all over and wipe my face with it."

"Carl, I agree with Rob. I want a safe place to leave my towel on the floor without having to worry that Rip might have shagged it."

"Okay, boys. I understand. He's not your dog, and the thought of accidentally wiping another dog's cum on my face would disgust me as well. I can put up with it with my dog but not anybody else's. I will spare you that, boys; I'll leave him with my stepfather. He could do with a break, as well as extra food.

"You don't have to sign off either; it's completely off the books. I'll bring you up every fortnight to sign on and you can see Rip then as well."

Anyway, we all agreed it seemed like a jolly good idea, so off we went on our next adventure. And what an adventure it turned out to be...

Mad Mick's Place

We left our little village early on a Sunday morning. I sorted Rip out with my stepfather, put what little clothing I had into carrier bags, gathered all my rave tapes together, and packed up my stereo player. We arrived at Mick's house early evening; he opened his front door as we pulled up outside. I was surprised at how small he was; I expected a big burly fucker. He was about my height, five foot eight, but had a lot more meat on him than me. He wasn't fat though; he looked fit for his age, which Simon reckoned was about sixty, but he could pass for fifty. He had thick red hair that was wild and unkempt, and a curious look on his face, as if he was sussing you out all the time. When we jumped out of the van, he looked me up and down, from my feet to my head, in that order, as if he was sizing me up for a coffin, and then he did the same with Rob.

"Nice to meet you, boys, but it doesn't look like there's a day's work in any of you. What the fuck have you brought me, Simon? They look like they belong on Top of the Pops."

He had a thick Irish accent but spoke softly and with authority.

"Mick mun, not in front of the boys. They've got feelings; if you prick them, they bleed."

"Prick them. They'd probably like it by the looks of the pair of them."

At this point, Mick's wife, who'd been observing us quietly in the background, spoke up…

"Mick, behave yourself. Don't listen to him, boys, he's just showing off. I'm Rose. Nice to meet you. Are you hungry? We've been waiting for you to come down to have dinner. Hope none of you are vegetarians."

"Vege-fucking-tarians? It looks like they haven't had a decent meal in years. I don't think they'll be fussy, love."

"Leave them alone, Mick. You'll scare them off."

We looked over at Simon for some sort of backup or explanation.

"Don't worry, boys, his bark is worse than his bite. He's a big softy, really."

"Woof, woof. *Woof*!" Mick barked.

Simon was laughing his head off. We didn't know what to make of it all. Rose nudged me and said…

"Come inside, boys. Now, Mick, none of that silly nonsense and be nice to your guests. Otherwise, you'll have to cut your toast into little soldiers yourself in the mornings."

She looked at us both and whispered…

"Don't let him intimidate you, boys; he's only messing with you. Underneath that very dull exterior, he's a big softie at heart. I wouldn't have married him otherwise."

Rose was right about Mick, although he looked and sounded like a right little tough fucker, and he *was* a tough fucker. He did have a softer side to him though, and when he laughed, he laughed like a pixie, but when he spoke, it was short and to the point; he didn't mince his words, and sometimes, we couldn't work out if he was joking or not until he started his little pixie giggles. Rose was indeed a cracking cook and she rustled up a lovely Sunday roast for us. She was younger than Mick, 'though not by a massive gap, but I couldn't guess her age because I'm shit at things like that. She was a little bit plump but not overweight, and when she smiled, her eyes would smile too; they would sparkle.

She made us feel at home and welcome. She liked talking about the Philippines and how beautiful her little Island of Boracay was. You could tell her heart was still in her Filipino roots. She told us they planned to make enough money to sell all the houses and retire to the Philippines, but they had experienced lots of delays with planning permission, surveyors, and solicitors. There were eight houses in total spread across the plot, each in various stages of completion. Mick listed the different stages but I won't bore you with the details. Some were fully built and just needed decorating inside, others only had the foundations laid, and the rest were somewhere in between. This is why there were a lot of different contractors on site doing all sorts of stuff.

There was one fully completed building but it wasn't a house; it was a community centre of all things, although the community never used it or had access to it. Mick was a bit vague on the details but, from reading between the lines, it seems he built it to get funding from the local council or to scam the local council into thinking he was providing something for the community. Mick's house was a quaint little cottage, a proper old stone building. Rose told us it used to be the village church a very long time ago but it had been converted into a house before they bought it. We were about a mile from the nearest town and there wasn't a bus stop nearby, so the options to get into town were walking, catching a taxi or getting a lift down.

Our caravan was opposite the community centre, out of Mick's earshot but not out of his sight. Rose gave us a guided tour of the place. The community centre was fully kitted out with a kitchen, a canteen, toilets, shower cubicles and little offices. We all agreed it would be a good place for a rave.

The caravan was a proper luxury one, probably a bit too luxurious for us. They had originally bought it to move into when all the houses had been built because they also planned to sell the cottage, then eventually sell the caravan and fuck off to the Philippines. The living area was spacious, with a big L-shaped couch that doubled up as a few beds; there were even fancy cushions.

The windows were huge and let in plenty of natural light. The kitchen had everything you would expect a kitchen to have; we even had a microwave, a toaster, and a little dining table. There was bread in a bread bin, milk and butter in the fridge, and tea, coffee, and sugar in the cupboards; all the bare essentials we needed. There were three bedrooms; a master bedroom, which Simon claimed straight away, and two smaller rooms, but they all had a double bed and wardrobes.

There was also a shower but Rose said we were to use the shower in the canteen block because she wanted to keep it in pristine condition. We were allowed to smoke in the caravan; Mick was a smoker as well, but he didn't smoke dope. Rose said she would clean it once a week when we were at work. The only other thing she told us was to make sure we take our muddy boots off outside the caravan and not to sit on the furniture in our work clothes, but other than that, she told us to treat it as our own home. Rob asked her how the food situation worked, and in her own words...

"The canteen will be open from nine o'clock every morning, five days a week. I serve a full English breakfast for anyone who wants one. They all have to pay mind, but you lot won't have to. Mick wanted to take it out of your wages but I told him that they deserve to be fed for free if they have to put up with you. I stop cooking at twelve o'clock but I'll make you all something for dinner and you can warm it up in the microwave when you finish work. I don't cook on the weekends, so you'll have to fend for yourselves. You can use the canteen or cook in the caravan. Gus prefers to cook in the canteen. Every Sunday, I make roast dinner in the house, and if you are not out partying or too drunk to eat, then you are all welcome to join us. Just let me know beforehand so I know how many to cook for, and I can make sure Mick will be on his best behaviour."

"Do you do all that on your own? The cooking, the cleaning and looking after Mick?"

"I do have an assistant, a local girl from the town. She doesn't do the looking after Mick bit though. I'm the only bugger that's daft enough to do that."

Then she left us all to unpack. But not long after that, Mick called in to see us. He sat down and said…

"Right, boys, I don't give a fuck what you do in your spare time; that's none of my business and what I do in my spare time is none of your business. Just make sure whatever you are doing or taking doesn't stop you from turning up for work in the mornings."

"What are the hours?" I asked him.

"Well, that depends on what needs doing and when it needs to be done, but your day will always start at 7 o'clock in the morning, no matter what."

"Does that include weekends?"

"You'll have two days off a week. They'll normally be the weekend, but sometimes they won't; it all depends on what needs doing and when it needs doing."

"So it's £250 a week, cash in hand, yes?" Rob asked.

"That's right. Is that enough money to buy whatever drugs you lot are on?"

We all burst out laughing.

"I'm sure it will be plenty, Mick," I said.

"Can we bring people back here?" Rob asked.

"As I said, you can do what the fuck you want in your own time; I was young once, so I know what it's like to have a hard-on and not have anywhere to stick it, so if you want to bring girls back here, or boys if that's what you are into, then it's fine by me. Just make sure that you turn up for work in the morning, and if they're handy with the shovel bring them along with you. And one other thing boys, don't you be bringing the police up here. I don't want them fuckers sniffing about the place so if you are going to get yourselves into trouble, just make sure you don't get caught."

As we were talking, Gus opened the door. We didn't know it was Gus then, but Mick said...

"Ah, Gus, come and meet our new recruits."

He looked over at us.

"Yeah, I know what you're thinking, Gus, but if it doesn't work out, we'll bury them under the foundations like the last ones."

"Which one of you is driving the dump truck?" Gus asked us.

Rob stuck his hand in the air as if he was in school...

"Me; Carl can't drive."

He looked over at me.

"Can you use a shovel, Carl??"

"Yes, of course I can, and a fork."

121

"What music are you into, boys?"

"We're into rave music."

"What the fucks rave music?"

"It's hard to explain but you'll hear it soon enough," Rob said.

"I fucking hope not. You lot better not keep me awake at night. Mick, if these fuckers are noisy neighbours, you're going to have to move my caravan away from them."

Mick looked us up and down again.

"I'm sure they'll adhere to the rules; nobody wants to upset their site manager. That would be an unfortunate thing to be doing when you work on a building site."

Simon and Gus talked about tarmac, kerbs, and materials. They both seemed to be on the same page; it sounded boring as fuck to me. Simon was in his element.

Just before they both left, Mick turned to us and said…

"One more thing, boys. When you start tomorrow, my boy Patrick will sort you out with everything you need, and don't be telling him you like drugs and prostitutes. He doesn't like that type of talk."

"Fuckin hell, Mick, what do you take us for? We are not some sort of cult."

"Well, you look like a bunch of cults to me."

And that ladies and entlegem was mad Mick and his long suffering wife, Rose. Now I'll tell you a little bit about Gus, who I mentioned earlier.

Gus

Gus was thirty years old. He was a proper heavy metal head with long blond stringy hair; he was a tall fucker, about six foot two, and he carried it well. He had a rugged, worn-out look on his face and looked quite serious most of the time. He loved his drink so when he wasn't working, he'd be down the Railway Tavern, sitting in the same seat every night and drinking the same drink, bow and black. He had been working with Mick for around ten years on various projects or scams, depending on how you look at them and which side of the fence you sit on.

He was a proper workhorse and loyal as fuck to Mick. And no matter how drunk he got the night before, he would always be up at six o'clock in the morning ready for his shift, and he'd be the first person on-site in and the last to leave. His job was to make sure everyone on site was doing their bit and getting the job done, as well as ordering materials or any machinery Mick needed. He could turn his hand to anything; sometimes, he'd do a bit of bricking, then maybe a bit of plumbing or carpentry, and he didn't mind being the labourer if someone needed one. He loved his heavy metal as much as we loved rave music; he was hardcore in his own right, been to all the concerts, did all the partying, and collected all the T-shirts. He didn't mind the odd joint now and then but not every night. He wasn't a man of many words but he was a straight talker when he did talk. He didn't bullshit or have any hidden agenda, and you knew exactly where you were with him. One of the jobs Mick assigned to Gus was to make sure we got up every morning and turned up for work on time. I think that ended up becoming the most frustrating task for him; he used to get so pissed off with us about it, and he was funny when he was pissed off so we used to play on it and fuck around with him.

A Rude Awakening

At six-thirty the following day, we were woken up by Gus banging like fuck on the caravan door; luckily, we had locked it, otherwise, he would have dragged us out of bed. He even went around every one of our bedroom windows, knocking on them. We got up, took turns to wash, and then made some tea and toast. Then off to work we went.

Mick's son was waiting for us outside. We knew who it was straight away because he looked like a mini version of Mick. He even spoke like him. He introduced himself to us as the health and safety officer and told me and Rob that we needed an induction before we were allowed on the site. We thought he was joking at first, but that was where the comparison to Mick ended; he was a very serious man indeed, and he wasn't joking at all. Simon didn't need an induction, though, so he went with Gus to work, work, busy, busy, work, work, bang bang.

He had us lifting breeze blocks, making sure we were picking them up correctly, wheeling a wheelbarrow and telling us about all the dangers on a building site. He asked us for our shoe, waist, and chest sizes and wrote them down. He said he would buy us some steel-toe cap boots and proper work wear and the money would be deducted from our wages. That was cool because we didn't have a lot of clothes anyway, so it would save us from wearing our going-out clothes to work as well.

He pointed out the fire exits in the canteen and the assembly point outside in case of a fire. Before he let us onto the site, he gave us a lecture on drugs. I'm not sure if he did that with everyone or if it was because of the way we looked. He said that if any of us were caught smoking or taking any drugs on the building site, we would face disciplinary action and possibly dismissal. I was half expecting him to pat us down or strip-search us. The whole experience was weird as fuck, even for us. He was as mad as Mick but on a different level. Anyway, I am not going to bore you with all the work shit we had to do because it was boring as fuck and we didn't like any of it. Simon was in his element; in all fairness, he knew his stuff and how to organise people, resources, concrete, and kerbstones.

For the first few weeks, we worked like fuck seven days a week. So much for the promise of two days off every week. We didn't get any more pay for it either, but Mick said he would sort us out with any extra money he owed us at the end of the contract; he said to think of it like a savings account. But the work wasn't hard and

Rose really looked after us. She would do all our laundry, change the bedsheets, and make sure we had clean towels and stuff; Rip would have loved all those towels. We looked forward to her Sunday dinners as well; we were like a proper family around the dinner table. Mick pretended he didn't like it, but he enjoyed our company. And sometimes Rose would cook a proper traditional Filipino dish for us to try. She promised us that one day, she would take us all to see her beautiful island of Boracay and meet her family, and she also promised us that when the contract finished, she would make sure Mick paid us everything we were owed and a little bit extra for putting up with him.

We liked Rose; she would take the piss out of Mick all the time, but in a kind of loving way. It was fun to watch his reactions and it revealed a lot about him. He was a loveable rogue and he was lucky to have Rose because no fucker else would put up with him.

Gus was relentless in his pursuit of waking us up every morning. We could set our clock by him. In fact, we didn't have an alarm clock; we had a Gus clock to wake us up. He even got a key cut to the caravan so he could let himself in and physically drag us out of bed. He certainly took every job he had seriously. We could see why Mick had employed him for so long; he was a thoroughbred workhorse. He'd get shit done and although he was quiet off-site, on-site, he was like a different person. He was fully in control of every fucker that stepped foot on his patch and made sure that no fucker was shirking or taking the piss.

One day, he sacked two brickies on the spot because they weren't bricking fast enough. That's where our bouncer skills came in because they started kicking off at him. We spotted what was happening and stood next to him with shovels in our hands. I was so glad they fucked off peacefully in the end; I don't think I could have hit any fucker with a shovel.

Gus worked hard and drank hard, and had the same routine every night; as soon as he finished work, he would eat his food, have a shower, shave, and comb his hair. We always knew when he was combing his hair because we would hear him whistling, and then he'd sit and wait for his taxi to arrive to take him down the Railway tavern. Then, not long after chucking out time, he would arrive back in a taxi. Sometimes Mick would get a phone call from the Railway Tavern because he'd fallen asleep and couldn't get a taxi home or the taxi drivers refused to carry him from his chair to their car, so Simon would have to go down and pick him up, or Rob if Simon wasn't able to. But as I said earlier, no matter what state he was in or what time it was when he came home, he would always be up in the morning at six o'clock and be banging on our door at six thirty.

We were all too fucked to go anywhere. I wasn't used to working, let alone seven days a week, but every night we would get stoned, listen to music, and talk about raving and what raves we would go to next. We even introduced Gus to our music. He said it sounded like two skeletons in a biscuit tin having a wank. A few of the West Wales crew would call up to see us and keep us updated on the rave scene and what was going down. But all work and no play makes Carlos a dull boy. So let's go and play again in the next chapter…

Dreamscape & the Hitchhiker

The next big rave we wanted to go to was Dreamscape 3 in Milton Keynes. It was an all-nighter. We had never been to a Dreamscape before and hadn't been to a big rave for ages, so we were very much looking forward to partaking and indulging ourselves. It was a good line-up as well:

Groove Rider

Fabio

Sy

Carl Cox

Top Buzz

DJ Dougal

Simon couldn't come with us because it was his girlfriend's birthday and she wanted him to spoil her, so he was taking her away for the weekend. We told him she was getting a bit too high-maintenance for our liking. He was borrowing Mick's car, so Rob asked Mick if we could have the company van. His reply was as follows:

"Don't be daft, you silly fucker; you haven't got a licence and I've seen the way you drive a dump truck. I don't mind you popping to the shop in it but driving over the bridge is another matter, and I don't want the police sniffing around my business if you get caught."

We tried to convince Simon to ditch his plans with his girlfriend; we told him that we thought he could do better and that she might be cheating on him, but he saw straight through our desperate attempts, although I think we did plant a seed of doubt in his head. We even asked him if he would hire a van for us but, like Mick, he didn't want to take that risk, which was fair enough because you never really know what might happen; we didn't either. So, in the end, we bought an old banger from a ganger working for Simon. It was a brown Allegro; £100 we paid for it. It didn't have any tax or MOT, but it was driveable and it was diesel, so we could fill it full of red. The rave was on a Friday night so we also needed to finish work early because it was a four-hour drive to Milton Keynes. Mick wasn't happy about that, and neither was Gus, but we had spoken to Rose beforehand and she sorted it all out for us, convincing him that we needed a break. We liked Rose; she had our backs. Mick even gave us his Road Atlas of Britain before we left and mapped out the journey for us. Page 32, E44.

The rave started at eight, so we left Wales at three o'clock. Five hours later, we were lost somewhere near

Norfolk. It was starting to get dark as well. I was panicking but Rob was taking it all in his stride; I wanted him to panic as well, then maybe he would see the urgency of our situation. I said…

"Rob, we need to find the nearest town or shop and ask people for directions."

"Carl, I told you earlier, I'm not going anywhere near any town because, as you know, I haven't got a driving licence and I'm not insured to drive. If the coppers pull us over, we'll be fucked and none of us will be going to any rave. I'll stop in the next lay-by, then we'll both make an effort to read the map and understand it this time."

"Well, there was a map on the back of the flyer but you ripped that bit up for roach material. I keep telling you not to use flyers for roaches."

"You smoked the joint as well, Carl, and you watched me doing it."

"We should be preserving flyers, not destroying them. They'll be worth a couple of quid in years to come."

"Well, they shouldn't put the maps on the corners of the flyer; they should leave that space empty. They know we are all smokers and we'd use anything for a roach in an emergency."

I spotted someone thumbing a lift just ahead.

133

"Look, there's a hitchhiker over there. He looks like a raver as well."

He was only a youngster; looked about the same age as us or a little bit younger. He was wearing a bucket hat and dungarees, and had a big rucksack on the floor next to him. He looked like he was thumbing a lift to a rave.

Rob pulled over. I leaned out of the window and said...

"Alright, mate, are you going to Dreamscape?"

"No. I'm going to Liverpool."

"Do you know where Dreamscape is?"

"Never heard of it."

I showed him the flyer.

"Oh, yes, I know where that is; it's down by B&Q and MFI."

"How far is it from here, mate?"

"About 15 miles, not very far. Do you want me to jump in? I'll show you."

"Yes, fuck I. That would be fucking brilliant, mate."

He jumped in the back, struggling to get the rucksack in. Rob looked at him and said...

"It's getting a bit late to be thumbing a lift; you might as well come to the rave with us. Have you got a tent in that rucksack? You could pitch it up in the car park."

"I'd love to but I can't afford it. I haven't got much money."

"You don't need any money to get in there; I'll show you how to get in for free. I don't usually take on apprentices but I'll make an exception for you because you helped us out and one good deed deserves another. And you might find someone there who's going to Liverpool in the morning."

"What time does the rave finish?"

"Seven o'clock, but not on the dot."

"Okay, but I'll still need some spending money. Do you want to buy any clothes? All Brand new. Still got the tags on."

He opened his rucksack and started laying out clothes on the back seat.

"Bit of a shoplifter, are you, mate?" Rob said to him.

"No, they are all my clothes but I've never worn them. I brought them with me to sell."

"It's okay, boy, we're not the police,"

"What clothes have you got? Any rave gear?" I asked.

"Yes, I got T-shirts, hats and jumpers."

"Gis us a look. I could do with some new T-shirts."

The back seat looked like a market stall display. He was definitely good at packing. He had shit loads of clothes in there. I spotted a Stussy T-shirt and a hat.

"What size are the T-shirts?"

"They are all my size; they'll fit you both."

I bought 2 T-shirts and a hat for £20 and Rob bought two hats for a tenner.

We arrived at the car park just after 9 o'clock, so we were only an hour late. Now, at this point, I have to say that the hitchhiker did tell us his name but I can't remember what it was and neither can Rob, so I will call him Danny because he reminded me of Danny Kendall from Grange Hill. He had thick black hair, a funny nose, and a strange-looking face, but he was nice enough though. We explained our rave rules to him like we had told everyone else; once we were inside, we split up. I certainly didn't want to be looking after him and neither did Rob. We could just about look after ourselves. Rob explained to him how we would attempt to get in and some other stuff about fences, walls, and security guards. He wanted to leave his rucksack in the car but we didn't want that because it meant we might have to wait around for him in the morning. So we put it under the car instead so he could easily grab it in the morning without having to wait for us or us having to wait for him. I went to join the queue and they fucked off to look for a weak spot in the security.

Now, I can't remember a lot of details after that, if I'm honest with you, but what I do remember is listening to DJ Dougal, and the music went off. The whole place went silent; it was surreal. For a brief moment, I remember thinking everyone was going to have a downer. There was going to be a big stampede and people would get crushed to death, and it was going to be on the news, but then the next thing, the whistle posse made some noise, and then the horn posse made more noise, and everyone was dancing to the sound of whistles and horns. And when the music came back on, the place erupted. I only saw Danny once. He was sitting against the wall with a load of other people in the chill-out area. He looked a bit pale and he was gurning. I went over to see him…

"Are you okay? Are you feeling alright?"

"Yes, I love it here."

"What have you done?"

"A Mitsubishi."

"Make sure you drink plenty of water. Are you sure you're okay?"

"Yes, everybody is really nice. They all keep giving me water."

"How did you and Rob manage to get in?"

"Get in where?"

"To the rave?"

"We dug a tunnel under the fence."

"Have you seen Rob?"

"Yes, he bought me a burger."

He put his hand in his pocket and showed me a beef burger, well just the burger bit first, then he brought out the bun part."

"Okay, I might see you later, or I might not. Take care and drink plenty of water, but not too much."

I didn't see Rob all night but it didn't worry me. It would have been good to have seen him but I knew that whatever he was doing, he was doing it in true hardcore style. The music stopped at about 8 o'clock. I hung around inside for a while, chatting with people, and then headed to the car park. It took me ages to find the car; I only spotted it in the end because I noticed Danny's ruck-sack propped up against the front grill and he was sitting next to it, waiting for us. I sat down with him. He told me he had never been to a rave before and it was the best experience of his life. I didn't realise it was his first-ever rave. As we were chatting, or more like as I was chatting, Rob came bouncing over, still off his chops. I knew straight away that it would be a while before we would leave the car park by the state of him. The thing with Rob was, he never wanted to leave a rave until everyone had gone and even then, he was always looking for another party to go to. He sat down with us and said he managed to get on the stage when Carl Cox was playing but he was booted off by one of the other dancers. He looked over at Danny...

"You look fucked. Are you okay?"

"Yes, just feeling a bit tired, that's all."

"Did you find anyone that was going to Liverpool?"

"No."

"What's in Liverpool anyway? Why are you heading up there?"

"My uncle lives in Liverpool; I'm going to visit him."

"I'll tell you what, you go and lie down in the back of the car, and we'll go and see if we can find anyone going to Liverpool."

He jumped into the back seat and off we went.

I explained to Rob that it was his first rave and I was a bit concerned that he had never taken a pill before, and we'd encouraged him; enabled him even.

"Look, Carl, he's not a kid. He had a rucksack full of stolen goods so he's not exactly innocent either. Shall we take him home with us?"

"Are you for real?"

"Yes. He's not going to Liverpool. He's a fucking drifter mun, and we can't just leave him here in that state; we brought this on him, Carl."

"I thought you just said that he's old enough to make his own mind up."

"I didn't say that."

"Well, you didn't say those exact words but you meant the same thing."

"Carl, what I say and what I mean are two different things. You should know that by now."

"What about Mick? What are we going to say to Mick?"

"Mick will be alright, mun; he could always do with an extra pair of hands on the site. He won't have to pay him the same as us."

"What about Rose?"

"She'll love him, mun. He might even be able to help her around the house."

"Where's he going to sleep?"

"In with us; we can turn the settee into a bed for him every night."

"You're fucking serious, aren't you?"

"Carl, we can't just leave him here, can we? What if he collapses in a ditch somewhere and dies? Or even worse, what if he hitches a lift and gets murdered?"

"Let's go and ask him then."

Rob was right. Danny jumped at the chance of coming home with us and even perked up a bit. He was still quiet but seemed happier; more relaxed and alert. It was a long journey home, we were all fucked, and there was no way Rob should have driven; he was still a bit off his chops. The bonus thing about the journey was that it turned out that Danny was a dab hand at rolling joints so we crowned him our "chief joint maker."

We finally arrived home at about five o'clock, snuck Danny into the caravan, and decided to tell Mick and Rose about him the next day when we had clearer heads. Simon was still away so we told Danny he could sleep in his room then we all went straight to bed. The following day, we got up, made some tea and toast, and chatted with Danny to explain the situation about Mick. We didn't go and tell Mick straight away; we wanted to find out more about Danny first but he was a bit cagey whenever we asked him for any personal stuff.

This is all we found out about him:

First Name: Danny

Last Name: None given

Age: 19

From: Birmingham

Address: No fixed abode

Family: Comes from a big family

Work History: Labouring on building sites

Hobbies: Listening to music.

But we could tell he was a good person who'd probably had some trouble in his life, and we respected his privacy. We've all got a past that we sometimes want to forget or get away from for a while. After breakfast, we decided to go and tell Mick, instructing Danny to stay quiet until we came to get him. When we got to the house, Mick and Rose were just finishing their breakfast; we sat down and explained the Danny situation. Rob was really selling it to Mick as an opportunity to have a bit of cheap labour around. Rose was more concerned about him hitching a lift and was glad that we had the sense to bring him home with us. Anyway, in the end, with Rose on our side, we convinced Mick it was a good thing. Rob went over to the caravan to get Danny. Mick gave him the same once-over look he gave us when we first met him, and then he said...

"What's your name?"

"Danny"

"Where are you from?"

"Birmingham."

"What have you done?"

"A Mitsubishi."

We both burst out laughing.

"He means what work have you done," Rob said.

"I've worked on building sites as a labourer."

"Running away from something, are you?"

"No. I've just been travelling around, visiting different friends and family."

"Have you got any friends or family in Wales?"

"Not that I know of."

"Where were you heading before these idiots picked you up?"

"To Liverpool; I was going to visit my uncle."

"Okay, I'll tell you the same thing as I told these fuckers; I don't care what the fuck you do in your spare time, as long as you turn up for work every day and you don't bring the police to my house. And don't go blaming me if these lot turn you into a Snack head."

We burst out laughing again, and even Danny and Rose laughed at that.

"I think you mean smack head, Mick," Rose said.

"Fuck knows with these lot. God knows what they do on the weekends. Now fuck off and leave us alone."

"I'll cook you all a lovely dinner later. Do you like all the vegetables, Danny?" Rose asked.

"I don't like any vegetables, only potatoes."

"Well, we'll have to do something about that. You got to eat plenty of greens."

Anyway, we thought that went well. We introduced Danny to Gus. The only thing he said was…

"It doesn't look like there's much work in him."

Simon came home later that night; we introduced him to Danny and told him the story. He was pissed off with us that we let him sleep in his bed, so they didn't get off to a good start until he could see how good Danny was at rolling joints. We got up for work the next day and left Danny in Patrick's capable hands. Patrick gave Danny an induction and took his vital statistics.

When he got on site, Gus gave him a wheelbarrow, a shovel, and a brush, then told him to clean the place up and help the brickies out when they needed bricks or a mix. We carried on with our usual boring work shit. At one point in the day, I noticed Danny was struggling with the wheelbarrow but it didn't have many bricks in there. I kept a bit of an eye on him after that, and I spotted a few other things that made me think he had either never worked on a building site before or that he was still fucked from the weekend. When we finished work that day, he was knackered. We had food and a shower, and he fell asleep on the settee as we were talking to him. We tried waking him up to make it into a bed for him but he was out cold so we chucked a blanket over him and let him sleep while we got stoned. A few of our friends called up as well and he slept through it all.

Things hadn't improved workwise by the middle of the second week. In fact, he was becoming a bit of a hazard on the site and the other workers were complaining about him getting in their way or being in the way. He didn't go to sleep straight after work but he wanted to get his bed set up by ten and he'd be fast asleep by half past ten. He was the fastest person to fall asleep I had ever known and when he did, it was a deep sleep; luckily, he didn't snore. But fair play to him, he would roll us enough joints to keep us going for the rest of the night before he went to sleep.

He wasn't good in the mornings either. It took ages for him to get out of bed; he was always the last one up and out, and he was pissing Gus right off. Gus called him "Danny do fuck-all" because he couldn't do fuck-all. In the end, he had enough of him and told him he couldn't work on the site anymore because he was a danger to himself and to others. Mick wasn't too pleased about the situation either. He wanted to get rid of "Danny do fuck-all" but we convinced him to let him stay and help Rose around the house and in the canteen. We told him Rose was looking a bit tired and she could do with the extra help and more time to relax. Rose agreed with that idea because she took pity on Danny and she also agreed that an extra pair of hands around the place would be helpful.

Everything was okay for the next three days. Gus was happier that he didn't have the stress of getting Danny out of bed or that he might cause an accident on site, Mick was pleased that Rose had more time to look after him, Rose was pleased she had someone to talk to about her beautiful Island of Boracay, and we were happy all the time anyway. But then, on the fourth day, Mick asked us all to call over to his house for a chat about "Danny do fuck-all"; without Danny being present, of course. Rose and Mick were sat at the table; they looked very serious and we could tell whatever was about to be said wasn't going to be good news. Rose opened first…

"Danny is a runaway; he's running away from home. He's not nineteen, he's only just turned 17."

"What do you mean? He told us he was nineteen and he was just drifting about."

"He was lying; he's lied to us all. He was drifting about but people were probably looking for him; his family or possibly even the police."

"But you can leave home at the age of sixteen; that's not running away, is it?" I said.

"Yes, but his parents are still legally responsible for him until he's eighteen."

"So how do you know all this then, Rose? Did he tell you?" Rob asked.

"Yes. As soon as I saw that boy, I knew there was something going on inside; he looked troubled. So I sat him down and asked him and he told me everything."

"So why is he running away from home?"

"Well, he says his mother has got a new boyfriend; he's moved into their house with his 18-year-old son, and Danny has to share his bedroom room with the son, and he hates him. So he decided to leave home without telling anyone."

Simon was laughing. He looked over to me and Rob and said…

"Fucking hell, boys; you kidnapped him and put him to work. That's jail time, that is, and they'll probably put you on rule 43."

Mick got up and said…

"I told you fuckers not to bring the police to this house, but not only will you bring the police, we'll have social services here, child protection and fucking Sky News parked outside if he stays any longer."

Rose chipped in…

"I told him he should be with his family; they're probably worried about him. I offered to phone his mother but he said they didn't have a phone in the house and he couldn't remember any other phone numbers. I don't think he's being honest about that but he obviously doesn't want to go home. But I told him he needs to let somebody know that he's safe."

All eyes were on me and Rob. I said...

"Look, we brought him here so we'll sort it out. We'll have a proper chat with him when we get back to the caravan. But I do agree he does have to go now, either way."

That night, Danny talked more than he ever did before. He opened up to us and apologised for lying, but he really didn't want to go back home and have to share his bedroom with anyone, and from the stories he told us, the mother's boyfriend sounded like a right wanker. We explained that he needed to tell somebody he was safe, so he eventually gave us his mother's phone number, but he didn't want to talk to her. We gave it to Rose straight away and she spoke to her. She then spoke to his uncle in Liverpool and it was all arranged that we would take Danny to the train station in the morning, put him on a train to Liverpool, and his uncle would meet him at the other end. So he spent the rest of the night rolling as many joints as he could for us.

The following day, that's exactly what we did, and that was the last we saw of Danny. Although we did make sure that when he reached Liverpool, he phoned us, and Rose spoke to his uncle. As a leaving present, we gave him all the joints he rolled the night before that we didn't smoke but we kept one joint behind as a memory to him. We said we would only smoke it in emergencies. That joint didn't even last the night.

The Night Owl

The weekend work stopped, thank fuck, and we found out there was a rave night in a club in Tenby called the Night Owl. It was on a Friday night and only a half-hour drive away, so that's where we started going every Friday. I loved the Night Owl; the West Wales crew were a mad bunch and we fitted in well with them. The music down there was more hard house than hardcore; that's why I loved it so much. The atmosphere was always bouncy and happy. Everyone was friendly and we became one big family. The one track that always reminds me of the Night Owl and, for me, captures the essence of the mood down there is…

New Atlantic – I Know.

Whenever I listen to that track, it reminds me of the Night Owl, the people, and the fun we had with them all. It also happens to be one of my all-time favourites. I loved dancing to that. Everyone loved Rob down there as well; he became a sort of guru. He'd get everyone going on the dance floor and always be on the stage or a table or the chairs. He was also the go-to guy if anyone was having a downer or a bad trip; he would cheer everyone up. It was hard not to come out of a downer when he was around. He was just so positive and happy and straight-talking, as well as off his fucking nut; he spread happiness around the place. He was even given a lifetime free entry pass into the club because the owners loved him and called him a "crowd pleaser". I was jealous as fuck. The only downside about Night Owl was that it shut at two o'clock, but afterwards, we would all head to the beach or whatever other party was going on. I used to love sitting on the beach and talking shit to people; everyone was so genuine and sincere. We would light a fire, sit around, walk down to the sea, dip our toes in, build sandcastles, or bury each other in the sand. It was just all fun and games. We were all so innocent and just enjoying life. So yes, I really loved the Night Owl and the West Wales crew; we made some really good friends down there and still keep in touch with some of them.

Upstairs Bathroom Water

I'm not sure how it happened, but one of the machine drivers on-site burst the water pipe feeding our caravan and the canteen, so we had to go to Mick's house for a shower. When Rob came back from his turn, he was holding a bottle of water in his hand and said...

"Fuck me, boys, have a drop of this. It feels like liquid energy; it fucking glides over your tongue, boys. I've never tasted anything like it."

I looked over at him. "Have you done a trip? Are you tripping Rob? How many fingers am I holding up?"

"I'm not fucking tripping unless there's something in this water. But honestly, boys, have a drop of this. You'll see exactly what I mean."

He handed me the bottle.

"What have you done to it? I'm not drinking that. You drink it first in front of me."

"I haven't done fuck all to it; it's from the tap in Mick's bathroom."

He took a sip, and his eyes rolled in his head as he was drinking it.

"Fuck me, boys. It doesn't just refresh you; it fucking renews you."

I grabbed the bottle off him and smelt it first to see if I could detect anything untoward in the scent. But I couldn't, so I took a small sip of it and then gulped it down. He was right; there was something special about it. I felt it flowing through my body and invigorating me. My legs, my arms, and even my mind felt refreshed.

"Fucking hell, Rob. I don't know if it's because you beefed it up or if we are smoking some really good dope, but I have to admit, that was fucking revitalising. I feel revitalised as fuck. It tingled my senses."

Simon shouted over, "Pass it here, you bunch of muppets; gis a drop."

I gave him the bottle. He took a sniff of it as well and once satisfied he couldn't smell anything untoward, he took a big gulp. He finished the bottle.

"Wow. That water must come straight from a spring or something. This is more than just water boys; it's an awakening. Mick is sitting on a goldmine."

"You mean shitting on a gold mine."

Rob grabbed the bottle off Simon.

"We need to fill it up again, boys, to see if it's a fluke or not. Carl, your turn next."

"Did you fill it up from the bath or the sink?" I asked.

"I had a drop of it from the sink first and straight away, I could tell there was something special about it, so then I tested it from the bath but it wasn't the same, and then I tested it from the downstairs sink as well. So, to answer your question, I got it from the upstairs bathroom sink."

I went over to Mick's house for a shower and to fill the empty bottle up. I took a sip straight from the tap in the sink and sure enough, I had the same feeling again; it was like a breath of fresh air in liquid form. Simon filled it up as well and it was exactly the same each time. Whatever was in that water did something to us; it was as if it had unlocked a hidden energy in our bodies. Later that night, we discussed at length why the water tasted so good. We figured that it must be pumped in straight from a spring or a well or something; it was like some sort of holy water. We had to give it a name and after much deliberation and arguing, we decided to call it "upstairs bathroom water."

The next day, we asked Mick about the "upstairs bathroom water" and if he knew where the source of the water came from. He said...

"There's something fucking wrong with you lot; it's normal fucking water, you daft twats. You've been smoking too much of that wacky backy."

"But have you ever drunk it yourself?" I asked him.

"Listen, boys, whatever fucked up shit you lot are on, I'm not interested, but if it makes you happy and you turn up for work every day, I don't give a fuck. But if you're going to be up and down my stairs filling up your bottles then just be fucking quiet and don't be doing it after midnight. And don't mention it to Patrick. You know what he's like; he'll have the environmental health people up here testing it."

We asked Rose about the water but she said she had never tried it and would never drink from any tap close to a toilet. We experimented using various drinking vessels, cups, glasses, and flasks. Rob even drank it out of his shoe and he reckoned it was just as good. So from then on, we only ever drank "upstairs bathroom water." We even used it for our tea as well so, as you can imagine, we were in and out of Mick's house a lot; but never after midnight, so we would always make sure that the last person to go over filled a couple of bottles up. Whenever people came around to visit us, we tested the "upstairs bathroom water" out on them as well, and every single person who drank it thought it was the best water they had ever tasted; one of the boys even used to bring his own empty bottles up for us to fill them up for him.

One weekend, Patrick and his family stayed in the house while Mick and Rose were away for the weekend.

We were in the caravan getting stoned when he called over to see us and as usual, he was talking about work, and he was boring the fuck out of us. I asked Rob to pass me the bottle of "upstairs bathroom water".

"What is upstairs bathroom water?" he asked.

Rob was quick off the mark with his answer.

"It's special water, Pat. We hid 200 acid tablets on top of the water tank in your father's bathroom and they fell into it, so now the upstairs bathroom water is trippy water; one sip, and it makes you trip like fuck."

"I do hope that's not true; that's very dangerous. Does my father know about it?"

"Well, have you noticed anything strange about him lately?"

"What do you mean strange? What type of strange? What does it do to you?"

"I'll show you now, Pat."

I took a big sip of the water and as I finished it, I started shaking my hands about and making funny faces and poking my tongue out at him; then I passed the water over to Rob. He took a swig of it and crawled on the floor on all fours, creeping like a cat and sniffing Pat's leg. Simon grabbed the bottle, took a swig, and started jumping up and down, making funny noises.

Pat didn't say a word; he just stood there watching us with a look of fear on his face. Rob picked up the bottle and said...

"Do you want to try some, Pat?"

"No, I certainly don't, and to be honest with you boys, if there is LSD in that tank, we need to get it drained. I don't think you should drink any more of it either, and you shouldn't be keeping drugs in my father's house."

He left pretty quickly after that and we all burst out laughing.

About ten minutes later, his wife came charging into the caravan.

"What is in that water?" she screamed at us.

"What do you mean?" I said.

"The water in the bathroom. Pat said there was acid in the tank and you were all off your heads. I bathed the kids in it earlier."

We all just burst out laughing at her; we couldn't help ourselves.

"It's not funny, boys; I'll need to take the kids to the hospital to get them checked out."

We stopped laughing when we saw the seriousness on her face and realised she was panicking and shaking.

I explained to her we were only joking with Pat about the acid tabs in the tank; we were just having a laugh and we didn't think he would believe us. I took a sip of the water and passed it to the other boys to prove it. I even asked her to taste some if she wanted to but she refused. She didn't see the funny side of it at all. She slammed the door on her way out without another word. She never spoke to us again after that, and Patrick wanted to give us a disciplinary but Mick talked him out of it.

We decided that we wanted to share the love and take our "upstairs bathroom water" to raves with us, so we would fill loads of bottles up and hand them out in the car park and in the services. Everyone who drank it thought it was the best water they had ever tasted and that it revitalised them. Sometimes, we would give it to people who were having a downer and it would bring them out of it. Rob would bring people back to the van to taste it; some people even came looking for us to ask us if they could have some "upstairs bathroom water."

I do miss "upstairs bathroom water". Nothing has ever come close to it since.

Funny Money

The £250-a-week wages we were promised weren't exactly accurate. For the first few weeks, we were paid what we were told, but then it started getting less and less. Mick would say he had cash flow problems, so sometimes we'd only get £100 a week. Other times, he'd ask us how much we needed for "sex, drugs, and rock and roll" and give us whatever money we needed to party. We didn't mind much—we were still signing on the dole, which topped up our wages. Plus, we had a warm, comfortable place to live, were being fed, could bring friends over for a smoke (which we did most nights and weekends), and we were partying. We only really needed enough money to keep that going. It would've been nice to have extra cash for emergencies but we weren't into material things. We preferred the synthetic stuff.

One afternoon, Mick wanted a word with me and asked me to call over to his house. I sat down with him at the table and he said…

"I've got a little job for you. Do you fancy doing a bit of shopping for me?"

"Do you mean shopping or shoplifting?"

"Well, it's a bit of both, really. It is shoplifting but you'll be paying for it."

"Yes, I will be paying for it if I get caught. What exactly do you mean by shopping?"

"Well, I've bought some counterfeit money—a lot of it."

He put a wad of £20 notes on the table.

"Take a look. What do you think?"

I picked one up and examined it. It looked genuine to me.

"How much dodgy money did you buy?"

"Never mind how much I bought. Can you tell if it's fake or not?"

"It looks just like the real deal to me, Mick."

"Good. Let's go shopping then."

"What are we going to buy?"

"I'm not going to buy anything. You are."

"What do you mean?"

"I want you to test these notes out in a few of the big shops in town. They don't have those ultraviolet light things in the local shops and I want to make sure they pass the test."

"What's in it for me?"

"Well, if I give you a £20 note, you can spend it on whatever you like, as long as you give me £10 change back in real money."

"Is that how much they cost? A tenner for twenty quid?"

"Fucking hell, you're a quick learner. You'll go far in life, you will."

"Not if I keep bothering with you, I won't."

So off we went to town on a shopping spree. I went to four shops altogether, just to make sure, and each time, the dodgy notes passed the fluorescent light and pen tests. I bought loads of munchies, some water pistols, lots of fags, gloves, whistles, and some dummies.

For the next few weeks, on every payday, Mick would ask if we wanted to be paid in fake money or real money. We always took the fake money option because he'd pay us £250 in fake cash but would only pay us £100 in real money, so it was a no-brainer, really.

Rob Has a Downer

One Saturday night, we invited a few people to the caravan; I think there were about 10 of us all together, a few boys and some girls. One of the boys brought a Chillum up with him. We had never heard of a "Chillum" before; he reckoned it was the best way to smoke pot if you wanted to get really high. It looked like a small pipe but without the bowl shape on the end; it was more like a hollow wooden tube, like the type of thing a tribesman would use to smoke ground-up berries out of.

He made a little mix like you do for a bong, then he packed one end of the pipe, lit it up, and sucked hard as fuck on it; pretty much like you do with a bong. Rob liked the look of it straight away and insisted it was his turn next but, being a greedy bastard, he wanted to try it out neat with just dope. He nearly choked after sucking on it. My chest hurt just looking at him. We all had a go of it but with a mix; none of us were brave or stupid enough to do it neat. We did have a really good head off it afterwards but I don't know if it was because of the chillum or that it was good dope. We were all giggling like fuck, having proper fits of laughter. We didn't even know what we were laughing about but it was contagious; proper belly laughs, the type where you run out of breath and if you make eye contact with someone, you erupt into even more laughter. I looked over at Rob a few times and that's exactly what happened to both of us, but then all of a sudden, he stopped laughing. He looked like he had seen a ghost, or something frightened the fuck out of him. The colour drained from his face, he shot out of his chair, stood up, looked around at us all and then opened the caravan door and ran outside; we watched him through the windows, running into the canteen, and as you can imagine, that made us all stop laughing immediately.

We sat in silence for a while, not knowing what to make of what we had just witnessed. It was obvious something had spun him out and he was having some sort of downer moment. We had all been there at one point or another; it comes with the territory. If you play with fire, you are going to get burned, simple as that. It happened to me in Pulse with my fit and to Simon down his uncle's house. It can be very scary, not only to the person experiencing it, but to the onlooker as well. It completely ruined the vibe and brought us all down to earth with a bang, so everyone got up to leave. We didn't have to say anything to each other; we all knew the score because that shit is contagious and the energy it brings with it is dark. So it was just me and Simon left in the caravan, and Rob in the canteen having a moment of madness. The funny thing about it was that Rob always reckoned he could never have a downer because his head was too strong, and yet there he was having a fucking downer on dope because he was a greedy bastard.

I looked over at Simon and said…

"Shall we go and see if he's alright?"

"He'll be alright now, mun. He just needed some fresh air, that's all. It's his own fault anyway for being so fucking greedy."

"Did you see the look on his face? Wonder what he saw?"

"Well, whatever it was freaked the fuck out of him. I'm glad he ran out. Imagine if he'd have stayed looking like that; we'd have all had a downer."

As we were talking, Rob opened the door, but he didn't come in; he was clutching his stomach. He looked over at Simon and said…

"Take me to the hospital; I can't breathe."

"Don't be so stupid now, mun. You wouldn't be able to talk if you couldn't breathe."

"I'm serious boys. Something's wrong with my chest. I think I'm having a heart attack."

I walked over to Rob and grabbed his wrist….

"Let me take your pulse. I'll tell you if you are having a heart attack."

164

"Please just take me to the hospital, boys; I'm begging you."

His breathing was getting heavier and more laboured. We could see that he was deadly serious and no amount of comforting words from us would convince him otherwise. The thing about Rob was that he was a stubborn fucker and once he got an idea in his head, there was no talking him out of it. Simon grabbed the car keys and off we went. I had to help him walk to the car; he was like a frail old man gasping for breath. He sat in the passenger seat and curled up into a ball, like a baby in the womb. I sat in the back seat and he held his hand out to me. He wanted me to hold his hand so I took hold of it and his breathing calmed down a bit. The hospital was about twenty miles away from where we were. We all sat in silence as Simon drove. Every now and then, Rob would shiver as if someone was walking over his grave, and he would squeeze my hand tighter as it happened.

After about ten minutes, Rob said…

"Water."

I rummaged around the back seat but couldn't find any.

"There's fuck all to drink in here. I cleaned the car out today so try not to be sick, will you, Rob?" Simon shouted over.

"Water," Rob said again.

"We'll have to stop at a shop," I said.

"There are no shops for miles; the nearest place to get water is Pont Abraham services, and I'll have to take a detour. Can't you wait, Rob?"

"I need water now. I can't breathe. I need water."

"Simon, you're going to have to stop. I'll knock on someone's door and ask them for water, fuck it." I said.

He stopped outside a row of houses; they all had big, long paths to the front doors. Rob jumped out and sat on a wall, still clutching his stomach. I got out of the car and Rob held his hand out to me. We both walked up the garden path, hand in hand. I knocked on the door and we waited for what seemed like ages; Rob couldn't stand up any longer so he was on his knees, with me still holding his hand. I knocked a little harder because I could hear the television. After the second knock, a man answered. He looked at me, and then his eyes followed my hand down to Rob, kneeling on the floor.

"Could I have a glass of water, please? My friend can't breathe."

He just stared at us for a bit.

"Okay, wait here a minute."

And then he closed the door. We didn't know if he was coming back or not so we just waited. Then the door opened again and he passed me a glass of water. Rob snatched it from me and gulped it down in one go. As soon as he finished it, the man grabbed it out of his hand and shut the door. I wanted to ask for another glass of water because I was getting thirsty, so I knocked again. But this time, he shouted…

"Go away. My wife has called the police."

Rob got to his feet, let go of my hand, and headed straight back to the car. My mouth was starting to dry up. There was a lamppost outside the house; I could see frost all over it. I scraped my fingers into the frost on the lamp-post and licked it off just to get a tiny bit of hydration to my lips. I did it a few times to get as much as I could. When I got back to the car, Rob was back in his curled-up position and he held out his hand again.

Simon looked at Rob and then over to me…

"Can we go back home now?

"No, I still need to go to the hospital."

By that time, it felt like we had been driving for hours but we were only five miles from the caravan. Just as Simon pulled off, I had a weird feeling come over me. For a brief moment, I felt like I was in some sort of cartoon world. I knew all too well what that feeling was; it was a prelude to a downer. I ignored it and brushed it off. There was no way I could dwell on it because dwelling takes you deeper. I squeezed Rob's hand unintentionally, thinking about trying not to think about it. He squeezed back and I could feel his negative energy transferring onto me. We both let go of each other hands at the same time; he knew he was passing it onto me, and I knew if I stayed in that car any longer, I would be in the same state as him.

"Stop the car. I got to get out." I shouted over at Simon.

"Are you serious?"

"Yeah, you need to stop the car. I'll walk home from here."

"Don't be so stupid. It's miles away and it's fucking freezing out."

"Simon, let him go," Rob said.

Simon stopped the car and I jumped out. It was freezing and I didn't have a jacket with me, but that was a small price to pay to save my head from the depths of darkness that would have been bestowed on me. I don't know how long it took me to get back to the caravan but it felt like weeks. I was freezing cold, my mouth was dry as fuck, and my lips were cracking. The upstairs bathroom water tasted better than it ever had before. Sometime in the early hours of the morning, Rob and Simon arrived home. Rob was his chirpy self and was breathing normally and laughing. Simon looked knackered. Rob sat next to me and said…

"Oh my fucking god, Carl, that was mad as fuck; I spun out big time. One minute, I could see everyone laughing and I could see your faces, and then the next minute, all I could see was everyone's teeth. None of you had a face, just big, massive teeth laughing at me, and then I started thinking, what is a laugh? And I couldn't work out what a laugh was, and the more I thought about it, the worse it was getting, and then my head went. So I had to escape from you all. So I laid down on the floor in the canteen because I felt hot and the floor was cold, but then I couldn't breathe."

"What happened when you got to the hospital?"

"A nurse examined me. I didn't tell her I was stoned; I said I was having chest pains, so she put me in a waiting room on a bed and went to get the doctor, but he was taking ages and I felt better then, so we came home. Did Duffin leave his chillum here?"

Paying Rob Out of Prison

We were sitting in the caravan one night when we heard a commotion coming from Mick's house. We looked out of the window at four police cars and a police van parked in the drive. Mick was on his doorstep shouting at the coppers. We all ran out to see what was going on. We could hear Mick saying...

"I don't know anyone by that name; you got the wrong fucking house. Now do me a favour and fuck off. You're scaring my wife and she's got a nervous disposition."

Rob approached the house first. He looked around and said....

"Having a party, are you Mick? You should have said; we would have invited some of our friends up."

The copper turned to look at Rob and a big smile broke out on his face; he said...

"Ah, Robert, we knew you were hiding down here somewhere; we've got a warrant for your arrest for non-payment of poll tax."

The copper put the handcuffs on Rob straight away.

"Aw, come on boys, no fuckers are paying poll tax. It'll be abolished soon anyway; it's a load of fucking shit."

"Look, Robert, I'm just doing my job; you'll have to come with us down to the station and then a unit will arrive to take you to Swansea prison. If you can produce the money to the courts to pay the fine, they'll release you, but as it stands now, we have to execute this warrant."

"How much is it?" Mick asked.

"It doesn't say on the warrant how much he owes."

"Can you go on your walkie-talkie and find out?"

"I'm sorry, but that's not in our remit; you'll have to contact the relevant people tomorrow and speak to them about any fees or payments."

And then the copper quickly and firmly placed Rob into the police van, and off they all fucked.

We were all gutted; we were due to go to Fantazia on the weekend and it wouldn't be the same without Rob. Mick was really pissed off that he brought the coppers up to the house and Gus was pissed off because he was one man down on the site. It put a right downer on things. The following day, Mick had a chat with us and said he would phone the relevant people, whoever they were, to find out how much Rob owed; we were kind of feeling hopeful that he might be able to pay the fine off. He told us all to fuck off to work and not to be skiving and moping about. We fucked off to the site but our heads and hearts weren't really in it; we couldn't imagine going to a rave without Rob. Around lunchtime, we went to see Mick to find out what he had found out. I asked him…

"What's the craic with Rob, Mick? Did you speak to anyone?" I asked.

"Yes, I did speak to some fucker; it took me a while to get answers though. He owes £180 plus costs incurred, whatever the fuck that means, so altogether, it comes to £450. I'm sorry, boys, but I can't afford to pay that amount of money for him; he will have to sit it out in jail."

"Did they say how long he would serve?"

"Aye, they said he would get the maximum sentence because he's been evading them. Ninety days, but he'll only serve half of that, so he'll be out in a month.

"Did you speak to him?"

"Yes, they let me speak to him. He said he'll sort out a visiting order for you as soon as he can, and he wants you to smuggle some dope in there for him. And he said to have a good time in Fandabidosies."

"I think you mean Fantazia, Mick."

"Fuck knows what he said. But what I do know is that I'm going to be a man down for a month and that's not good at all."

"Where is he now?"

"They transferred him from the police station early this morning. He's in Swansea prison waiting for them to prepare his room."

"How much pay have we got this week?" I asked Mick.

"I've only got £175 each for you this week, boys; I've had to pay a lot of cash out to those fucking brickies. I asked them to wait another few weeks but they said they would down tools if I didn't pay them."

"What about Rob's pay then?" I asked him.

"I'll give it to Rose to keep for him for when he comes out. Don't worry about that; it'll be safe with Rose."

"So what if we use Rob's wages and me and Simon chip in some of ours to pay him out?"

"You can do what the fuck you want with your money. I don't care."

So we started doing the maths. Rob had £175; we could use all that. He wouldn't need money to buy a ticket for Fantazia because he always snuck in, so all he would need is money for refreshments, and he didn't really need that at a push because he could buy his refreshments on tick from one of the Swansea boys. Gus even said he would chip in some money as well; he always had his full pay and it was going to be a nightmare for him

173

without a dump truck driver for a month, so it was in his best interests. So after doing the numbers, we agreed that me and Simon would chip in £100 each and Gus would chip in £75, giving us a grand total of £475.

We didn't waste any more time; Mick drove us to the courts in Swansea. We spoke to some guy who didn't have a clue what he was talking about. He told us we needed to go to the council offices, so we went over there and eventually, after speaking to about five different people, we found the right department and the person who dealt with paying off fines for non-payment of poll tax. We handed over the cash to them, they made a phone call to the prison, and said we were lucky because Rob still hadn't been processed through the system; if he had we wouldn't have been able to bail him out. Mind you, they did all that after they took the money; cheeky fuckers.

An hour later, we arrived at Swansea Prison. Rob was waiting outside with a massive grin on his face. Olay, Olay, O fucking lay. And off we went to Fantazia.

All Good Things Must Come to an End

One Monday afternoon, just after lunchtime, we were all busy on-site, working away, when Mick called down. He shouted something out, I couldn't quite work out what it was, and then he clambered on top of a stack of breeze blocks and said...

"Everyone, stop what you're doing. I've got something to say and you all need to hear it."

We all stopped what we were doing. It never took much convincing for us to down tools.

He continued....

"I've sold the business to one of my partners, lock, stock and fucking barrel. Everything must go, including you lot. I'm sorry, boys. You'll all get paid what you are owed; no fucker's going to lose out. Don't you be worrying about that side of things.

"When will we get paid?" shouted Bob the builder, or whatever his name was.

"My accountant is sorting it all out now in the house. By the time you pack all your shit up, he'll be ready for you. Come to the house, and you'll get what you are owed and a little bonus for the inconvenience."

And then he clambered off the breeze blocks, turned to us, and said...

"I want the four of you to call to the house at five o'clock for a meeting. Rose will cook you dinner; she's got a nice surprise for you."

We wasted no time at all downing our tools. We said goodbye to all the boys on site and fucked off to the caravan to discuss what just went on. Even Gus came back and sat with us, and he reckoned it was as much a surprise to him as it was to us. I don't think he was bullshitting either because he had a look of sadness on his face. We were all coming up with our own theories as to what might be going on; they were all batshit, but one thing we did all agree on was that Mick was a dodgy fucker so there was definitely something illegal going on. Anyway, five o'clock came and we headed over to see Mick to find out what surprise he had in store for us. We were hoping it would be a nice payoff of a couple of grand or maybe even one of the houses he was building. We had big dreams.

We sat at the table. Rose served us our dinner.

"So what's the craic then, Mick? Is this the last supper before you evict us?" I asked him.

"Well, I had an offer that I couldn't refuse. I won't get into the details because it's none of your fucking business, but after discussing it with Rose, we decided fuck it, we're going to sell up and move to the Philippines."

Rob turned to Mick and said…

"I'm really happy for both of you but I hope that's not your nice surprise because, although it is nice for Rose to be going back home and for you to be taking early retirement with a suitcase full of cash, it doesn't exactly thrill me."

"That's not the surprise. Tell them, Rose."

"I want to take you all to see my beautiful home in Boracay and Mick is going to pay. Isn't that right, Mick?" Rose said.

"Well, it's the least I could do, and you could do with a break from all the drugs and the boom-boom music; you look like fucking zombies. I don't mean you, Gus, but you could do with a nice break too, and the beer is cheap as fuck out there. In fact, everything is cheap as fuck out there, so it won't break the bank taking you fuckers for a little break."

Rose chipped in: "We'll go to Manilla first and stay there for a week because I want to do a bit of shopping and meet up with some friends. Then we'll all fly over to my little home in Boracay, and you can stay at my resort and meet my family."

"But before we go, I still need you lot to do a bit of work for me on site," Mick said.

"What do you want us to do, Mick?" Gus asked.

"Just tidy the place up and get rid of any shit that shouldn't be here. Nothing too taxing for you boys."

"When do we leave?" we all asked.

"In about two weeks, so if you haven't got a passport, you need to get one pronto. Rose will sort out all the flights and accommodation, so all you ejits need to do is give her your details and whatever else she needs to complete the forms. And I hope none of you are scared of needles because you're going to need a few jabs up the doctors to make sure you don't die out there from malaria."

"So you won't be coming back with us then, Mick?" I asked.

"No. I've made quite a bit of money from offloading this place but everything is getting so expensive these days and it won't last long, but out there, I can live like a King for the rest of my life, however long or short that maybe."

"Can we have a rave up here before we leave?" Rob asked him.

"No, you fucking can't. I don't want hundreds of little fuckers like you lot running around the place popping pills or whatever you call them. And while I'm on that subject, they don't tolerate any of that shit out in the Philippines. They'll put you straight in jail and believe me, you don't want to be in one of their jails; not even Rob would be able to handle it. So don't be taking anything out with you or be taking anything out there. Isn't that right, Rose?"

"Oh yes. The government or the police don't take kindly to people selling or taking drugs; it's not like over here. They won't ask any questions; they'll just put you in jail."

"Don't worry, Mick, I'll make sure they don't take any drugs with them and keep an eye on them out there as well," Gus said.

Mick then turned to us and said...

"Now fuck off, the lot of you, and don't you be using this as an excuse to get up late for work. There's still two weeks before we leave and you got a lot of shit to clean up."

We went back to the caravan. We were in shock but we all agreed it was a fucking nice surprise indeed and we couldn't wait for a holiday. We would be out there for about a month altogether, by the sounds of it. We were also a bit sad to be leaving Mick's place because we loved it down there, apart from the work bit. It was a good laugh, all living together; sometimes, we'd have our arguments about silly stuff, but we got over it. Not only that, but there would be no more "upstairs bathroom water."

Over the course of the next few days we tried to find out more about what deal Mick had made and how much money he had made out of it, but he was telling no tales. Rose did let slip a couple of things though. When Mick said lock, stock, and barrel, he meant it; he sold everything, even down to the contents of the house. They were taking nothing with them, only their clothes, and leaving everything else as it was. She wouldn't divulge exactly how much money he'd made, no matter how many times we asked her. The closest we got was she said it was over a million pounds.

The deal would take about two months to complete by the time all the paperwork was sorted but Rose insisted he get a big down payment off them, enough to go to the Philippines; she didn't want to wait around for the solicitors to sort everything out. She also let slip that they were having a little leaving party for family and friends so we managed to convince Mick to let us have our own little leaving party in the canteen for some of our friends. He agreed, as long as it didn't turn into a rave and we didn't bring the police to the house. We also asked him if he could add an additional clause in the contract that whoever owns the house has to allow us to call down periodically to fill our bottles up with "upstairs bathroom water" whenever required. He obviously took no notice of us and didn't contact his solicitors about it.

So, to cut a long story short, in those two weeks, we did quite a lot of cleaning up on the site. I went home to see Rip and let him know I was going on holiday. We went for a nice walk up the river, I told him what I had been up to, and he told me what he had been up to as well; he'd put on a bit of weight too, which was nice to see. My stepfather told me not to go to a foreign country with a man and a woman I hardly knew; he said there were a lot of kidnappings in that part of the world. I explained that Rob, Simon and Gus would be out there too, so it's not as if I am going on my own. He did have a good point and, to be honest, the thought had never crossed my mind until he mentioned it; neither did the kidnapping bit, which scared me the most.

Anyway, I phoned my auntie to let her know, and she told me to make sure I wear a condom if I go with any girls out there because there is a lot of AIDS in that part of the world. Then I visited a few of my friends to say goodbye and get their addresses so I could write and send them a postcard. They told me to be careful if I took any drugs out there because there was a lot of heroin in that part of the world.

So the three main things we were all scared of was getting kidnapped, contracting HIV or becoming a junky. We had our jabs, and me and Rob had to get our passports. That was all a bit of a drama. We had to have our photos signed but we didn't know who could do it for us. We took them down to the school we used to go to and asked the head teacher; we didn't make an appointment but just went down there and knocked on his door. He recognised us straight away as we had both been in his office quite a few times, but never together. He did say that we were an unlikely alliance but probably good for one another.

Anyway, our little leaving party plans were coming along nicely. We had put the word around town and told a few of the people back home, and most of them said they would come up to say goodbye. We set the canteen up and arranged a local DJ to play. We were due to leave on Saturday so we organised the party for the Friday night. By Friday morning, we were all packed and ready to leave the next day. We made sure to take plenty of rave tapes as we didn't know if there was a rave scene in the Philippines.

Gus decided he would go down the Railway Tavern for the night to say his goodbyes to the barman and the rest of the regulars. By late afternoon, people had started arriving at our party, and then later on in the evening, Mick and Rose's family and friends had turned up for their party. Patrick came and had a chat. He wished us all the best for the future and said to contact him if we ever needed a reference. That wouldn't be likely, though, because me and Rob planned to become DJs when we got back home, and besides, we needed a break after all that work we did. Both parties were in full swing by ten o'clock; there were about 100 people at our party and about 15 at Mick's. He did call over to see us once; we thought he was going to tell us off for inviting so many people but he was drunk as fuck and in a really good mood, saying he would have done the same at our age. He even had a little dance. We also made sure that we had plenty of "upstairs bathroom water" for everyone. It was very emotional for all of us; we knew we would see them again in raves, but we probably wouldn't see each other in between raves anymore. I made sure I got loads of people's addresses so I could write to them. Gus arrived home in a taxi just after midnight, joined us for a few hours and then went to bed. The last of the ravers left about six in the morning. We spent a few hours cleaning up after everyone and by ten o'clock two minibuses arrived to take us to Heathrow airport and onto our next adventure…

We're Leaving on a Jet Plane

The journey to Heathrow took about 3 hours so we all slept on the way there. We were fucked and knew we would be in for a long day and night. Rose said the journey to the Philippines would take about 24 hours all together because we would have to stop in Dubai and Hong Kong to wait for the connecting flights.

The first leg of the journey from London to Dubai was a 12-hour flight. As we boarded the plane, we were greeted by the stewardesses. They were all dressed in red, even red lipstick, and they looked beautiful; they had big smiles and were really helpful and friendly. Me and Rob fell in love with them all. Mick and Rose sat together; it was the quietest I had ever seen him. He looked like he was having a downer.

None of us were seated together though, for some reason; maybe it was cheaper, I'm not sure, but we were all within eyesight of each other, so we could have a chat. When the plane took off, it was cool as fuck. I loved it. I had never been on a plane before. We decided to have a drink and get drunk. We figured we were not going to be raving for a while so we might as well become pissheads. Gus had already decided that himself and was the first person on the plane to ask for a drink. The man sitting

185

next to me told me that Dubai had the biggest duty-free in the world. He also told me a lot of other things but that was the only thing I remember him saying.

Before we got to Dubai, the captain announced over the speaker that we were making an unscheduled stop in Abu Dhabi; the man sitting next to me said it was very unusual, which made me a bit concerned. I asked one of the stewardesses, and she told me it was just routine, which made me worry even more because the captain said it was unscheduled, and she said it was routine; their stories didn't match up. I wouldn't say we all panicked but there was certainly a bit of unease on the plane amongst everyone.

Looking out of the window, it seemed like Abu Dhabi was in the middle of the desert and, as it happened, that's exactly where it was. The airport looked tiny. As we got closer, we could see a bunch of people waiting on the landing strip; as we got even closer, we could see that they were all dressed in desert camouflage, and as we got closer still, we could see they were all heavily armed. There was an army waiting for us to land and that is when we all started to panic. Mick had woken up by that time, and I could see by his face that even he was a bit worried. When we finally landed someone on the ground pushed one of them big aeroplane ladders up to the doorway, the captain opened the hatch, a few of the armed soldiers got on the plane, and ordered everyone to get off. We did exactly what we were told, in an orderly fashion as well, and when everyone was off, another bunch of soldiers boarded; it seemed like they were looking for something or for someone. None of us were allowed to move; even the pilot was among all of us passengers and the guards were pointing their guns at us. An English guy in a suit was shouting at the general of the army, telling him that this sort of thing does not happen in the UK and we should all be allowed back on the plane. He seemed like some sort of ambassador or English counsel, the way he was talking and the words he was using; he was very official and shouting all sorts of constitutional stuff but it didn't seem to faze the general.

After a while the soldiers got off the plane, spoke to the general, and then he said we could all get back on. It was a bizarre experience; I thought that we were all going to be kidnapped. When we got back to our seats and prepared for take-off, the captain apologised to us but didn't explain what it was all about. Eventually, we landed in Dubai, gave all the stewardesses a big hug, and had a photo taken with them.

The next flight was to Hong Kong; we were all seated apart again but I had a window seat this time. Rose gave

Mick a sleeping pill to knock him out because he wasn't enjoying flying at all. It was a good thing he was going out there to live because he would never have made the flight back home. I sat next to a guy who said he was the Hong Kong rugby team manager. He also told me that I was in for a treat because landing at Hong Kong airport was one of the hardest and most challenging airports for a pilot to land; some pilots were unable to do it. That was the first time I felt a bit nervous. I didn't really like talking to him because he kept going on about other dangerous things about flying and planes, so I decided I needed to calm my nerves and I wrote a letter to some friends back home. In the end, I never sent that letter but I have always kept it so here it is in its entirety:

Well, hello, Donna & Alan, how are you? Good, I hope. I'm sorry I couldn't stay for long when I called down to see you, but everything was a mad rush; well, it was nice to see you both anyway. How are the girls? Good, I hope. Give them my love and the hamsters, too.

Well, at the moment, I am on a plane heading for Hong Kong. We just got off one plane from London to Dubai. It was a 12-hour flight, and I couldn't sleep at all; it was too uncomfortable. But the service on the plane was business. Loads of smart stewardesses walked up and down all through the flight, smiling all the time. When we got off the plane, we gave them a hug and took a couple of photos of them.

Anyway at the moment I've got a seat by the window, it's a brilliant view, I can see the ocean, and what looks like a massive patch of sandy coloured land, it's the biz, what a view, oh and I can see the wing of the plane and a flashing light at the end of it, the view out of the window though is beautiful, we are on top of the clouds. To the right of me, there is a man reading a book, or it could be a book reading a man; I'm not sure; I've got the headphones on.

All I can see now out of the window is the sea. I'm a long way from Wales, and everyone looks funny, even the bloke sitting next to me; who is he anyway? Ask about for me, will you? Oh, the plane is shaking now. It's good when it shakes. It's scary a bit, but that's what's good about it. Someone just said it's turbulence. As I was writing the word "turbulence," the plane shook again.

Anyway, I'll send you some postcards when we arrive, and if we end up staying out here to live, I will send you my address but make sure you write back because it would be nice to hear from you, but I know you would write back anyway so what I am on about? It's me, the one you got to worry about, who won't write back, but I

189

promise that I will try though, anyway I'm writing now so it shows that I think of you, but make sure that the both of you write, well I'm feeling tired now, but I don't know if I can sleep, but I'm going to try to give it a go, so I will close for now.Look after yourselves, the girls, and the hamsters, and don't forget to write. If you don't hear from me for a while, don't worry. I have loads and loads of people to write to, but you are on top of the list, so goodnight both. See you when I see you.

All the best – Carlos.

When we were about to land, the man next to me talked me through every stage of what the pilot had to do as I looked out of the window. We were practically flying right over the city and could see the rooftops and the cars just below us. Fair play to the skills of the pilot; everyone clapped when we landed. I think it was some sort of tradition if you were lucky enough to survive the landing; it was the first time I realised exactly why some people kissed the floor after landing. We didn't have to get off the plane in Hong Kong, thank fuck. They refuelled it or did whatever they needed to do and within an hour, we were back on the road again or in the skies again, more like. It was an uneventful flight, the food was shit, but we had more drinks. It was a short flight compared to the others, only about two and a half hours.

It was night-time when we landed in Manilla. As soon as we got off the plane, the heat and humidity hit us; none of us were dressed for that weather. Rose was very excited; she even kissed the floor when we got off the plane. Rose's cousin met us at the airport. He was wearing a white suit; the material was wavy, almost like pyjamas. He was tall and skinny and very excitable, bouncing around the place, almost dancing. He handed us a load of condoms, explaining that the condoms in the Philippines would be too small for our cocks. He was a funny guy and looked like someone who likes to party, so we asked him if there were any raves to go to in Manilla. He didn't know what a rave was but he said there was a nightclub near where we were staying that played "fast music". We figured that could be another name for rave music so I wrote the name of it down in my notebook. He arranged some taxis to take us all to the hotel; Mick and Rose had one taxi and we all jumped in another one. He didn't come with us, though. Rose said she would see him in a week in Boracay.

Manilla

Manilla was a sprawling metropolis; it was the busiest place I had ever been to in my life. The traffic system was chaos, there was no such thing as mirror, signal, manoeuvre; they just beeped their horns and turned whichever way they wanted to go. The taxi driver had to weave his way through traffic and every time we stopped, someone would come to the window and ask us for money. We only had British currency but they were happy to take that; we gave them everything we had on us. It was really sad to see all the poverty as we drove around.

We finally arrived at a very posh hotel with wide stone steps leading up to the entrance; there were armed guards positioned outside. Mick and Rose had already arrived and were waiting for us; Rose had to pay the taxi driver because we had given all our money to the people who were begging. The hotel inside was amazing; the floor was marble, it had big fuck-off chandeliers hanging from the ceiling, there were even statues inside and a fountain in the centre of the lobby area, and it was air-conditioned, which provided a welcoming breeze of fresh, cold, crisp air. We all sat down, except for Gus, who went looking for the bar. We were in awe of the place and couldn't wait to see what our rooms were like.

After about 15 minutes, Mick came and sat with us and said...

"Right boys, me and Rose are all booked in. Now, you can go and book yourselves into your hotel."

"What do you mean, Mick? I thought this was our hotel." I said.

"Don't be so silly, you daft twat. This place is too posh for you fuckers, and I don't want you bringing no police with guns to my room in the middle of the night."

"So where are we staying then?"

"It's just down the road from here. It's not far; the taxi driver will take you there."

He pointed outside and we could see our taxi driver. He waved at us and we all waved back.

"Don't worry, boys, it's a nice hotel; it's just not as nice as this one."

Then he reached into his money pouch and gave us all 500 pesos each. Gus came and sat down with us with a bottle of San Miguel. Mick handed him a wad of cash, which looked much bigger than ours.

"Right, now fuck off, boys and leave us in peace. Call over and see me tomorrow whenever you all decide to wake up. When you get to your hotel, just tell them you are with Rose, she has sorted it all out, and don't go fucking crazy on the room service."

Then off we all fucked to our not-so-posh hotel. It wasn't a bad hotel but nothing like the one Mick was staying in; it was a lot smaller, for starters. But it was clean, with a small reception desk, a bar, and a pool table. It also had armed guards outside. We didn't bother exploring or having a drink that night, we just all went to our rooms. Me and Rob shared a room and Gus and Simon had the room next door to us. It had been a very eventful forty-eight hours and we were all knackered; we fell asleep straight away.

The next day, I woke up at three o'clock in the afternoon, Manilla time, Rob was still sleeping. I looked out of the window and right next to our hotel was a little shanty town. There were about 20 huts built out of corrugated steel, all closely packed together. There were women cooking outside the huts, hanging clothes on the washing lines, and loads of kids running around; I had never seen so much poverty on that scale before. I woke Rob up to see it and he was as shocked as me. We just both felt really sad to see whole families living in huts. We also realised how fortunate we were; it really put life into perspective for us. The hotel we were staying in was posh as fuck compared to how they were living, and we had the cheek to complain about anything after seeing that.

We all went downstairs for breakfast. The guy at the reception desk said Mick had phoned and left a message for us. He wrote the message down and read it out word for word as follows:

"When those lazy bastards get up, tell them to call over and see me in my lovely posh hotel and don't serve them any beer with their breakfast."

We were too late for breakfast so I went for the spaghetti Bolognese; it was the only thing on the menu that appealed to me. Gus tried to order a beer but, fair play to them, they stuck to Mick's orders and wouldn't serve him. After we all finished, we headed off to see Mick and Rose in their hotel. The streets were full of people, there were beggars everywhere, and everyone was staring and pointing at us. It was weird as fuck; it felt like we were famous or something. When we got to Mick's hotel, the receptionist told us he was in the swimming pool on the rooftop. They were certainly living the high life already. Mick was drinking a bottle of San Miguel and Rose was sipping on a cocktail, and that was our cue to order our first drink; we all had a bottle of San Miguel each. We sat next to Mick and Rose. Mick said to us...

"Right, boys, this is the way it's going to work. We'll be in Manila for a week. You lot stay out of our way and we'll stay out of your way, and make sure you don't get into any trouble with the police because these fuckers have got guns and they will shoot you. You've all got more than enough money to keep you going for a week. Now off you fuck and enjoy your holiday."

Rose gave us a list of places she thought we should visit in Manilla. She said to just ask the taxi driver to take us there.

So once again, off we all fucked. Me, Rob and Simon ordered a taxi to take us to the nearest shopping centre; we needed to buy some clothes that suited the climate. We also needed to buy a ghetto blaster; we had loads of rave tapes but nothing to play them on so that was a necessity. Gus headed back to the hotel bar; he said he wasn't going to waste any of his money on clothes when he already had some. The shopping centre was busy as fuck. The taxi driver offered to stay with us and be our guide and interpreter, and although everybody out there spoke English, we took him up on his offer.

Everyone in the shopping centre was staring and pointing at us. Some of the women even touched Rob's hair as they passed him; the taxi driver told us that blond hair is a rarity in Asian countries, and blond men symbolise masculinity and are seen as sexually attractive. Rob liked that. We also noticed that a crowd of people seemed to be following us around as well. I'm pretty sure they thought we were some famous boy band or something.

People were also stopping Simon and asking him to show them his tattoos. They wanted to touch them as well. Nobody was interested in me; there was nothing about me that stood out. We all decided to buy the same clothes for a laugh; thin white jogging bottoms and a black T-shirt with a bright green palm tree on the front because we thought it looked like a cannabis plant. We went into the shop in our old clothes and came out in our new ones, all looking identical. As we walked out of the shop together the people outside started clapping; we definitely looked like a boy band now and were enjoying the attention we were getting. We found an electrical appliances shop and bought a ghetto blaster so we decided to test it out in the shopping mall and put on a little dance show for everyone. I had brought one of our mix tapes with me so I chucked it into the ghetto blaster and turned it up full blast. The first track that came on was...

Rozalla – Everybody's free.

It's a bit fluffy, I know, and some might scoff at it but, in my opinion, it was one of the crossover tracks that really worked in raves and the clubs. Anyway, we danced for about half an hour and the whole place stopped to watch. When we finished, everyone clapped, and some people even asked us for our autographs. I'm not sure who they thought we were but we loved it either way. The taxi driver took us back to our hotel and we gave him a massive tip for all his help. He said he would wait outside for us and take us wherever we wanted to go whenever we wanted, any time, day or night. We spotted Gus in a small bar next to the hotel. He was sitting on his own, sweating like fuck. There was a pile of empty San Miguel bottles on his table. I said to him…

"What the fuck are you doing out here? It's boiling. There's no air conditioning either."

He looked at me with his squinty eyes and said…

"It's only 10 pesos for a bottle of San Miguel in here; it's 12 Pesos in the hotel."

We all burst out laughing…

"You tight fucker. You'd rather sit out here sweating your cock off for the sake of 2 Pesos?"

"It's alright in here, mun; I can watch people go by as well. I like the view better."

"Fuckin' hell, you can hardly see *me*, let alone some fucker walking by."

We left him to it and had a few bottles of San Miguel in the hotel bar. Rob and Simon played pool, which I'd never been into, but I was happy sitting inside with air conditioning. I ordered another plate of spaghetti Bolognese, and Rob and Simon ordered some other weird stuff. We stayed there until early evening and then decided to find the bar Rose's cousin mentioned, so we asked our tour guide/taxi driver to take us there. Manilla was just as busy as the night before; there were people begging and prostitutes lining the side streets. We were all a bit scared, to be honest; we would have never been able to navigate around the place without help.

The taxi driver found the club and said he would come inside with us but sit out of the way; we told him to sit with us. It was empty inside. There was a small dance floor and a DJ booth in the corner. He was playing cheesy pop music and I had forgotten to take a tape out with me. We all got up to dance but within about five minutes the music stopped and we were surrounded by the bouncers, ushering us off the dance floor. They told us that groups of men weren't allowed to dance together, so we all sat down. The taxi driver told us that they don't like men dancing together because people coming into the club might think it was a gay bar.

Not long after, a group of women came and sat by us. There were about six of them, fit as fuck too; they sat on our laps and the taxi driver told us they were prostitutes.

We said to them that we didn't want to have sex but we didn't mind buying them drinks and having a chat. They were all very giggly and funny; we had a good laugh with them. We stayed there for the rest of the night, just chatting and not dancing.

We decided that night that we would stay local for the rest of the week and not venture into the city again. It was all too much of a culture shock for us—the poverty, the prostitution, and everyone staring at us all the time. I guess at that age, we were too young to appreciate the different cultures. It wasn't really scary out there but we were scared. There was so much we could have seen and done but instead, we decided to stay in and near the hotel where we felt safe and armed guards were outside. So for the next few days, we would meet up in the bar whenever we got out of bed, have some food, wash it down with a few bottles of San Miguel, then pop to the bar next door for a few with Gus; then we would all pile in one room and order room service until it was time to go to sleep.

We had a few different waiters bringing us our San Miguels, but one of them was funny and he liked our music and wanted to know all about raves. We liked him too. His name was Anton; he said it meant "worthy of praise", and we all agreed he was worthy of praise because he was a really hard worker. We made sure we gave him loads of tips every time he brought us our drinks. Sometimes, we would take the ghetto blaster outside the hotel and dance on the steps; people would gather around and clap, and they started calling us "New Kids on the Block." They would shout it out of the windows whenever they saw us. Rob gave the security guard outside the hotel a pair of his trainers because he noticed his shoes were worn. He asked him at first what his shoe size was so he could buy him a new pair but he said he liked the Troop trainers Rob was wearing, so he tried them on. He said they fitted him but they didn't look like they did, but Rob gave them to him anyway. It was funny to see an armed guard in full army gear outside the hotel, holding a rifle and wearing a pair of Troop trainers.

Two days before we were due to leave, Mick summoned us all to his hotel to talk about the travel arrangements from Manilla to Boracay. Rose was busy packing and singing along. She was very excited to finally go back home and couldn't wait to show us her beautiful paradise island. We sat down and Mick said...

"Right, boys; Rose thought I should give you the option before we book the boat for you."

"Boat? What do you mean boat? I thought we were flying there." I said.

"Well, I decided I won't be getting on another plane so we're going to book a nice boat trip over instead."

Rose chipped in, "It's a ten-hour trip by boat or about five hours by plane. It's completely up to you boys; it's the same price either way."

We all deliberated but not for long. None of us fancied going over on a boat, not for ten hours; we wanted to get there as soon as we could so we decided to stick to the original plan and fly.

So the day of departure finally arrived; we said goodbye to Anton and gave him whatever money we had left on us. We also gave him our mixtape, the one with Rozalla on it; he liked it the most. We met Mick and Rose at their hotel. Mick gave us another 500 Pesos each and then we went off to the airport. It wasn't the same airport we arrived in though; in fact, it looked too small for an airport. There was only one check-in desk, a few seats, and a vending machine; it looked more like a taxi rank. We were the only ones in the airport. We checked in and the woman at the desk cheerfully informed us that our plane was ready for departure, then pointed out the window. There it was, sitting on a small patch of tarmac—a tiny plane with propellers. The pilot was stood outside, waving at us like we were old friends. My heart sank into my stomach. The thought of being trapped in that rickety contraption high up in the sky for the next five hours filled me with a deep, cold dread.

Rob said straight away…

"I'm sitting by the pilot, boys."

I didn't want to sit anywhere on that plane; Simon and Gus thought it would be exciting, and I thought we were all about to die.

The pilot beckoned us over and gestured to the luggage compartment; we had to put our own suitcases into the plane, like you do on a coach trip. As we boarded, he shook our hands and gave us all a pair of earplugs. There were no designated seats; it was only an eight-seater plane, with no other cabin crew or air hostesses. As soon as the pilot got on the plane, Rob asked if he could sit next to him in the cockpit; he had no problem with that at all. There was a view of the cockpit wherever you sat on the plane. When we took off, the noise of the propellers was deafening; we could see why he gave us all earplugs. It wasn't a smooth take-off at all and I had never been so terrified in my life as we climbed up into the clouds; I just didn't feel safe at all in that little plane. I don't know why, but I kept thinking that the pilot might be on a kamikaze mission and crash into the sea and kill us all. I was absolutely terrified. I decided the only way to survive the ordeal was to make myself go to sleep, so that's exactly what I did. My fear basically flipped a switch and my body shut down for the entire flight. If I hadn't managed to put myself to sleep, every single minute in that plane up in the sky would've been like living through some sort of waking nightmare.

Beautiful Boracay

Somehow, with God on our side, we landed in Boracay about four o'clock in the afternoon. I didn't open my eyes until the plane was firmly on the ground; I was so happy that the ordeal was over and I was still alive. I knew we would have to do it all again in a few weeks but I put that thought right to the back of my mind. Otherwise, I wouldn't have been able to enjoy myself for the rest of the holiday.

We all got off the plane and grabbed our luggage. The first thing I noticed was the humid tropical air, and it all felt very relaxed and laid back, certainly compared to Manilla. The airport was in the middle of nowhere; it was barely a building, just a few wooden benches under a thatched bamboo roof. The woman at reception greeted us with a big smile. We went to give her our passports but she said she didn't need to see them; she just pointed in the direction of the way out. When we got outside, we were in a harbour surrounded by white sand curving along the coastline.

The water was crystal clear, palm trees were blowing softly in the breeze, and there were small fishing boats dotted around; it just felt so chilled out and laid back. A few locals offered to help us with our luggage; we said we could manage but they insisted. Rose's cousin met us outside the airport; he said he was going to take us to Boracay. We thought we were in Boracay but he told us we were in Caticlan so the journey wasn't quite over; we had to jump on a boat to get to Boracay, but it was only a 20-minute journey and the sea was calm. It was a fishing boat called a "Banca" that doubled up as a tourist boat. It was bright yellow, with green and red stripes, like the Bob Marley colours; it had large bamboo outriggers on either side to help it balance on the water, and a little engine. It was a relaxing journey; a bit bumpy at times but not scary bumpy. You could see the coral reefs in the sea; that's how clear the water was. We landed close to the beach and had to wade the rest of the way onto dry land. It felt like the perfect introduction to a getaway Island.

But the journey still wasn't over; the resort we were staying at was another few miles away and there were no cars or buses on Boracay. In fact, there were no roads and the main mode of transport, other than on foot, was by motorbike, so we each had to jump on the back of one. A few motorbike taxis were waiting for us; one of the riders took all our luggage and we rode pillion with the others. They didn't give us any helmets to wear and they weren't wearing any either. I didn't really enjoy that journey; the guy was driving too fast for my liking, and it was all on

sand, so we were all over the place. I think he was showing off and trying to impress me. I wasn't impressed; I
would have rather he had taken his time. Rob, Simon and
Gus loved it. Gus used to have a motorbike so he was in
his oils; they even had them all race each other to the resort.

When we finally reached it, Rose's family was there
to greet us; there were loads of them. Her mother introduced herself and put one of those Hawaiian ribbons
around our necks; it felt like we were in a James Bond
film. We couldn't believe the scene in front of us; it
looked like a perfect place for a honeymoon, with white
sands, palm trees, a clear sea and little bamboo huts. It
wasn't commercialised at all, with no high-rise hotels or
fancy resorts; there were small huts made out of bamboo
and driftwood, and it wasn't bustling with people, just
locals and a few backpackers wandering about. It felt so
serene and intimate. Rose was right; it was a beautiful
paradise island, untouched and unspoilt... wasted on us.

Once we'd met all her family, Rose's mother showed
us around the resort. It was on the beach; well, just off
the beach, but only a little bit. The floor was sand and we
each had a hut of our own. It had a small veranda with a
hammock and a few chairs, and reminded me of those
huts in the Tarzan films. There was a four-poster bed

made out of bamboo with a mosquito net draped over it but no air conditioning. Luckily, they'd just had electricity fitted so there was a small fan on the bedside table. There was also a shower but the water came straight from the sea so there were no temperature controls. There were little paths connecting each of the huts and I was in the front hut closest to the eating area and the bar. There were armed guards as well but they were sat on the beach on deck chairs.

We all put our stuff in our cabins, then Rose's mother cooked us a traditional Filipino meal while we waited for Mick and Rose to arrive. The restaurant area was all outdoors but with a wooden covering; it could seat about 20 people, the cooking area was in full view, and the bar was to the side. We really couldn't believe how beautiful the place was and how calming it felt after the hustle and bustle of Manilla. We all agreed that if any of us were to get married, we would have our honeymoon in Boracay and we would invite each other.

After our food and a few San Miguels, we went to check out the beach; the water was lukewarm and crystal clear. There was a Chinese man lying on an air bed; he looked a bit like Mr Miyagi from the karate kid, same size and shape and the same beard. He looked wise as fuck and at peace with the world and himself. When we had all had enough of the sea, we went for a walk around the island. People were looking at us but it wasn't as bad as in Manilla; they'd have a glance and then carry on with whatever they were doing. There were a few family-run resorts along the beach so we had a drink at each one. They were all very welcoming and genuine, authentic people; they reminded us of ravers and made us feel like family. We could see why Rose loved the place so much. We went back to the resort just in time for Mick and Rose's arrival. All her family and friends had gathered to greet her, and the look on her face was priceless. It was as if she had just come up off a pill; it was that look of pure joy and overwhelming happiness, just like a double dove. Mick looked fucking exhausted. We all had a few drinks and then it was time to go to bed. Rose promised to show us around the rest of the island the next day. My bed was comfortable; I made sure the mosquito nets were all tucked into the mattress so there were no little gaps for the mozzies to get in. I hate creepy crawly things. I fell asleep straight away.

I have no idea what time I woke up the next day but I did have a nice long sleep. I decided to try the shower out; it was lukewarm and the water was salty but I felt refreshed after it. Mick, Rose and Gus were already up and eating in the restaurant. Rob and Simon arrived not long after me. Rose had taught the chef how to make a full English breakfast so we all had one, washed down with a few San Miguels. After breakfast, Rose had arranged to show us around the local village so we all went for a day out. We each had to jump on a motorbike taxi to get there; it was funny as fuck seeing Mick on the back of a motorbike, arms tightly wrapped around the rider, telling him to slow the fuck down. It was weird to see Rose as well, but she looked like she had done it hundreds of times.

The village was quite busy, with lots of market stalls. Rose bought us all each a pair of flip-flops because we were still wearing our trainers, which wasn't practical, especially when walking on the sand all day. She took us to her favourite restaurant and insisted we try a traditional dish called Kare-kare, which was a beef stew with a peanut sauce; it looked more like a curry than a stew but the owner said that its name means "curry." Rose told us that if something is really good in the Philippines, they often say its name twice, so Kare-kare sort of meant really good curry. Afterwards, she took us on a boat trip around the cove to see a bat cave; not Batman's cave but a cave that bats live in. I didn't really fancy the idea because, like I said, I don't like creepy crawly things, especially with wings, but it was cool. The cave was massive;

the boat drove straight into the middle of it, and the ceiling of the cave was covered in bats, like hundreds of them, if not thousands. The driver was shining a torch up at them and all I was thinking is that what if he wakes them up with the light and they start flying at us like the flying monkeys in the Wizard of Oz. We didn't stay in there too long though, thank fuck.

When we got back to the resort, we chatted with one of the waiters about where to go to dance and party, and he told us there were two clubs that were quite busy. One was called "Beachcombers", the other one was "The Bazura Bar", and they were both on the beachfront. So that's where we headed that night. Gus had planned to stay in the restaurant getting pissed for the duration of the holiday because he didn't have far to walk to his cabin, but we convinced him to come with us and at least try it out once. Both clubs were close together but were about a mile from our resort, so we had a choice to walk or catch a motorbike taxi. We decided to walk along the beach to do a bit more exploring. Before we left, I grabbed a rave tape from my room

Easygroove in Fantazia, New Years Eve 1991-1992.

It was our favourite rave tape and we listened to it more than any other tape. Personally, I think that set with DJ Lisa has to be the best set ever played in a rave; it's just full of raw energy and gathers momentum with every track. You can feel the atmosphere every time you listen to it, pure raw energy, and the MC gives a shout-out to the Swansea Crew as well. Everything about it is perfect. It was one rave we were always gutted we missed. That and Castle Morton.

Anyway, I was hoping I could get one of the DJs to put the tape on for us so we could listen to it on a proper sound system and get on the dance floor; we were missing that feeling. We got to the "Beachcomber" first. The tables and chairs were on the beachfront, and the bar was under palm trees. They were playing reggae music, little tiki lights and lanterns lit the place up, and it had a tropical island vibe to it. A few people were sitting down, mainly tourists; some looked really posh, while others looked like hippies and backpackers. It felt like the type of place where really rich people go for holidays and hippies go for a retreat or to get away from the rat race. The dance floor was the beach, the backdrop was the sea, and the lights were the sky. It was table service as well, so we all sat down to enjoy a few bottles of San Miguel and basked in the beauty of Boracay. Rob got chatting with a

212

few people and asked if they had any dope; they all told him the same thing: that it was dangerous to be talking about drugs in the Philippines. He reckoned they did have dope on them because he could smell it but they must have thought he was an undercover cop or something. The Bazura bar was only about a five-minute walk down the beach but didn't open until nine o'clock, so we had a few more beers while we waited. Gus was well impressed with the "Beachcomber" bar. He picked his seat and said…

"This is going to be my local from now on, boys, and this is my seat. You lot can go wherever the fuck you want but I'm staying put."

We all fucked off to the Bazura bar at about ten o'clock and left him to it.

The Bazura bar was on the beachfront as well, but it had a proper structure, kind of like an island shack. It was an open-air bar, as in it didn't have a ceiling. It was a lot busier and livelier than the Beachcomber. It also had a proper dancefloor, a wooden one, and a DJ booth above it. As we walked into the place, the DJ was playing…

CeCe Peniston – Finally.

We knew straight away we were going to like it there, and it was going to be our local club. The music was pop, with some light rave tunes going on, but people weren't moving much. They were on the dance floor but weren't getting into it and soaking it up. It looked a bit like the nightclubs back home where all the girls were dancing around their handbags and the boys stood on the outskirts of the dance floor watching them, although there were some boys dancing in little groups, so at least that was allowed. Anyway, we had a few more drinks, and then the DJ played...

Nomad – (I Wanna Give You) Devotion.

We all headed to the dance floor like we were on auto-pilot and that was when everyone stopped to look at us, giving us space to dance and just staring at us for a while. But then we beckoned them to join in and slowly, they all started dancing again but also watching us at the same time. I climbed up to the DJ booth and asked him if he would play our tape, which he was more than happy to do; I think he thought we were in a band and I was handing him our album to play. He stuck it on straight away. In fact, he stopped the music and didn't even bother mixing it in. The whole place went silent, and then the next thing we heard was…

You're in tune to the sound of Groove. Easygroove is in the house.
You haven't heard hardcore yet until you've heard Groove, Easygroove Easygroove.

Rob jumped up on the podium in front of the DJ's booth. Everybody froze and just watched us, but then they slowly started dancing again. I don't think any of them had heard proper rave music before, and they certainly didn't know how to dance to it. We could see them trying to copy our moves; they watched us to see how we danced and then tried to do the same. I could see a little bit of Rob, a little bit of Simon and a little bit of me breaking out in people as they danced. The DJ played both sides of the tape and asked me if he could make a copy of it.

We stayed on the dance floor all night. We really needed it after Manilla and everything else, and it felt good. It was the first time we had ever been drunk and danced to rave music in a club; we even spoke about just getting pissed at our next rave back home but that was just drunk talk. It was about 3 o'clock when it closed and there were no motorbike taxis about, so we walked back home along the beach. As we passed the Beachcomber bar we noticed it was closed but Gus was still sitting in the same seat, sleeping. He was the last man sitting. We managed to wake him and get him home.

The next night we headed down to the Bazura bar a bit later because Rose threw a bit of a party for us in the restaurant. We decided to take the beach walk again and Gus came with us. We dropped him off at the Beach-comber and headed straight to the Bazura bar. As we were approaching the place, we could hear our Fantazia tape playing…

Whose flying with ecstasy airwaves. Whose flying with ecstasy airwaves.
Come on, get those hands up in the air.
Reach for the sky. Reach for the sky
Easygroove making you high.

Our hands were in the air as we walked in. We looked around, and the place was rammed; the dance floor was packed. It was definitely a lot busier than the night before. When they all noticed us, they stopped dancing and started clapping and cheering. Even the people who weren't on the dance floor were clapping for us. We felt like celebrities; what a fucking rush that was. We joined them on the dance floor and Rob got up on the podium. The girls weren't dancing around their handbags anymore, and the boys weren't standing on the edge of the dance floor. They were all dancing like hardcore ravers; it was as if we had lit a fuse and set the place on fire. Some of them would dance beside us, trying to copy our moves. It was fucking mental. We brought the place alive and changed the way they danced.

The next week was pretty much the same. We'd get up in the morning or afternoon, have some breakfast or lunch with Mick and Rose, then we'd go down to the beach and drink a few San Miguels. When night fell upon us we'd head to the Beachcomber for a few drinks with Gus, then over to the Bazura bar for a dance. We made a few friends out there as well. They were all very welcoming and always happy to see us. We got friendly with some girls who worked behind the bar. They were a few years older than us, and they were lovely and easy to talk to, and genuinely interested in our stories. We loved hearing about their lives, especially what it was like to grow up in Boracay.

After the bar closed, we'd all sit on the beach and chat for hours. They were down-to-earth; there was no falseness about them. They were worldly-wise and could hold a good conversation. They had a good sense of humour and were always laughing at the things we would say, even when we weren't trying to be funny. One night, they even asked us to marry them. At first, we thought they were joking, but it turned out they were serious. They wanted to move to the UK to escape poverty. Simon told them he already had a girlfriend, but me and Rob did consider it for a while. But we just couldn't figure out how to go about it and it seemed like a lot of hassle. We didn't really have stable lives back home; I wasn't even paying any of my bills, Rob was always being evicted, and none of us had jobs. It would be like taking them from one difficult situation to another and, more importantly, if we did marry them, they might want us to stop going to raves, so we had to decline the offer, tempting though it was. We felt really bad about that because they were genuinely lovely girls, but they understood and it didn't spoil our friendship with them.

One afternoon, we all hired motorbikes; it was Gus's idea and Rob and Simon were well up for it. I wasn't because I didn't know how to ride a motorbike; they had all ridden one before but I had only ever been on the back of one and I never liked that experience, but I felt a bit of peer pressure from the others. We hired them off the motorbike taxi boys. They didn't even want to see our passports or a driving licence; in fact, they were all putting in a sales pitch about whose bike was the best to hire.

"Take my bike. It's faster than his bike."

"You want good comfortable seat? My bike is best."

Eventually, after they'd all haggled with each other, we settled on a price; I can't remember how much it was but it was cheap as fuck. As we were leaving, the girls from the Bazura bar pulled up on their bikes. They said they would take us on a tour of the mountains to a secluded cove, so off we all went. Except for me; I needed help to start my bike and pull off. All the motorbike taxi boys were laughing at me, and when I did pull off, the back wheel was sliding in the sand and I kept stalling. The rest of them all fucked off, except for Rob. He held back, not so much to watch out for me but more to laugh at my efforts to try to ride a motorbike; he knew I had never ridden one before and he wanted to see the shit show I would make of it. I didn't disappoint him. I chose the smallest bike as well but it was still a bit too big for me. I couldn't balance it properly; I couldn't balance myself properly or work out the revs, the clutch or the brakes. I fell off a few times as well and had to pick the bike up. Luckily, it was soft sand but it was a very stressful ordeal for me. Funny for onlookers as I passed them though; I provided a bit of entertainment for anybody who saw me.

Eventually, I sort of got the hang of things but it didn't go very fast. Rob had his amusement and was off racing with the rest of them, leaving me to fend for myself. At one point, I lost sight of them all for about ten minutes and shat myself; I thought I was going to get lost in the jungle. I caught up with them, well, the sight of them anyway, and eventually, we all parked up. The two girls got off their bikes, stripped off naked in front of us, and ran into the sea, shouting for us to follow them. I had no intention of going into the sea; I was just happy to get off the bike for a while. Rob was the first to strip off and run in after them, and then Simon stripped off, and Gus followed, but he kept his pants on.

I walked slowly down to the beach with all my clothes still on. I watched the girls dive off a rock and swim into the cove, with Rob following suit, while Simon and Gus jumped in from the rocks. Rob struggled a bit as he resurfaced; the sea wasn't calm, and there were a few waves bashing against the rocks. He managed to compose himself, then they all followed the girls into the cove and I lost sight of them for a good five minutes. I was thinking that I might never see them alive again, that the girls had lured us to the cove to kill us, and now they would have to kill me. I would have been easy to catch as well, if I tried to get away on the motorbike. But they eventually swam back out, then we all sat on the beach for a while. Rob, Gus, and Simon got dressed but the girls sat there naked. It felt really weird but that was the best part of the day for me. Anyway, I was glad when it was all over and we returned the bikes.

There was one night Simon wasn't feeling too well, so he stayed in the resort. We all thought he had malaria; he was sweating like fuck and shivering, and he said he had forgotten to take his malaria tablets. Rose assured him it wasn't malaria but he was too ill to come out. So me and Rob went to the Bazura bar without him. At one point, Rob was at the bar for quite a while, and when he came back, he said…

"I think I can get us some speed."

"From who?"

"I was just talking to some girls by the bar. I asked them if they could get any dope but they don't know of any. But they reckon they can get something called "Shabu", and by the way she described it, it sounds like speed but it gives you a high like an E."

"I don't know about that, Rob. I don't think we should; it's too dangerous out here and we don't know what we are buying, and who are these girls? They might rip us off?"

"Don't be so paranoid, mun, they're just two girls; they sound genuine enough. We don't have to give them any money now. They said they'll take us to someone to buy it off and just give them a bit of money for sorting it out."

"Fucking hell, Rob, that sounds even more dodgy."

"Come on, mun. I'll try it out first and if it's any good, you can have some then."

"How much is it?"

"She said it was fifty pesos for a bag. I think it's a gram, but I'm not sure. That's only about a pound in our money. It's fuck all. If you don't want any, I'll go on my own."

"Fucking hell, mun Rob. You can't go on your own. Come on then."

He introduced me to the two girls, then we each jumped on the backs of their motorbikes and they took us deep into the jungle. The further we went, the more the trees closed in around us, and the path got narrower and wilder. We were miles away from civilisation, heading straight into the unknown. I was shitting myself; I was thinking all sorts of things, like they were taking us to a gang of men that would beat us, rape us or murder us...

or all three. We eventually came to a stop outside a secluded wooden hut. The wooden slats of the front window were open and there was a soft light coming from inside. A woman came to the window; she was completely topless. We all got off the bikes and the girls went over to chat with the woman, telling me and Rob to stay where we were; they spoke for a little bit and then called us over.

I looked at Rob and said...

"I'm not going in that place. I'll wait outside."

"Well, if I don't see you again, Carl, it was nice knowing you."

And off he went into the wooden hut with a topless woman and two girls that he had only met an hour before."

I was left outside on my own in the middle of nowhere in the pitch black. The only light around for miles was the little glimmer of it coming from the hut. About ten minutes passed and there was still no sign of them coming out. I could see movement in the hut and could hear Rob's voice but then I couldn't hear him for a while. Then the three of them walked out together. I was so relieved to see that he was still alive, although he was a bit unsteady on his feet.

"You alright, Rob?"

"Carl, mun. Yes. I'm cool."

He looked stoned as fuck, but a different kind of stoned that I had seen him before; I didn't like the look of that type of stoned on his face or in his eyes."

We all jumped on the bikes and headed to the Bazura bar. When we got inside, Rob sat down straight away; he was sweating like fuck and could hardly keep his eyes open. I was starting to get worried because he wasn't speaking either; he was just slumped in the seat.

The girls said he would be alright, I gave them a few Pesos, then they fucked off pretty sharpish. I never saw them again after that. I didn't know what to do with Rob. Other people were noticing the state on him as well, so I said he was drunk. I asked one of the girls behind the bar to help me to get him down to the beach. I told her what had happened and she knew straight away what was going on. She told me that shabu was the street name for methamphetamine, otherwise known as "Crystal meth" or "crack". She said he needed an hour or two to come around but he should be okay after that, so I sat on the beach with him until he was back to normal. When he was able to speak coherently he told me that he had "chased the dragon" in the hut, meaning he smoked the shabu off some tin foil and inhaled it. The topless woman insisted he try some out in front of her. I didn't want anything to do with that shit and I made sure that he threw the rest of it away.

The day before we were due to leave, Rose and Mick organised a leaving party for us; it was quite sentimental because we would probably never see them again. In the evening, we went over to the Beachcomber and the Bazura bar for the last time and said goodbye to everyone; that was quite sad too. We had become good friends with the girls and knew we would probably never see them again either. We gave them whatever money we had left, swapped addresses, wished them all the happiness in the world, and told them if they were ever in Wales to look us up. I didn't sleep at all that night because I was worried about the plane journey home.

In the morning, we set off for the airport. We all cried as we said goodbye to Mick and Rose. When Mick wasn't looking, Rose gave us an envelope each; it contained £500, not Pesos.

I was shitting myself at the thought of being in that little plane and hoped I still had the power to make myself go to sleep again. The other boys weren't too fussed about it; Gus wanted to sit by the pilot on the way home. We got to the airport and were the only passengers again. We waited about half an hour for our little plane to land on the gravel but it wasn't the same one we arrived in; it was an older model and looked a bit more battered, which made me feel even worse. We had to load our luggage into it again, and the pilot shook our hands and gave us earplugs. Gus sat in the front with him and we sat wherever we wanted. As the engine started I was willing my body to knock me out. We didn't move for a long time but the engine was revving like fuck and the pilot looked a bit worried. After a while, he got out of his seat without turning the engine off; he looked at us and said…

"You need to push the plane off the gravel. The wheels can't move; the plane is stuck."

At first, we thought he was joking, but he fucking wasn't. We all had to get out of the plane and push the fucking thing onto harder gravel so the wheels could get a grip. That really did it for me; I was sure we were all going to die. We eventually got back on the plane and finally took off. I knocked myself out again not long after we were in the air and we landed in Manilla safely; I kissed the floor this time. We caught all our connecting flights and arrived at Heathrow at eleven o'clock at night. We booked into a hotel, me and Rob shared a room, and Gus and Simon had the room next to us. We all went straight to sleep; Gus didn't even have a drink.

The Rave in Mick's Place

We all woke up early the next morning. Simon had arranged for his uncle to pick us up and take us home to Wales; he was looking forward to seeing his girlfriend. Gus had already arranged a job working away; he was up hours before us and we were glad he didn't wake us up. Me and Rob decided we didn't want to go home quite yet and had a cunning plan to go back to Mick's place for a while, given he still owned it for a few more weeks. The plan was to have a rave in the community centre, which was big enough to hold about two hundred people and was deserted. Mick wouldn't know fuck all about it so there would be no comebacks. Simon's uncle dropped us off just after the Severn bridge and we hitchhiked the rest of the way to Mick's.

When we got there, everything was exactly as we left it. The first thing we did was break into Mick's house to have some "upstairs bathroom water" but the electricity and the water supply had been cut off; we were gutted. We still had keys to the caravan so we let ourselves in, but there was no electricity or water there either. The gas bottles were full and still working though, so at least we would have heat, a cooker, and a bit of light from the gas fire. We popped down to town to buy some normal water and make a few phone calls, and by eight o'clock in the evening we were sitting in the caravan with our mate Matt, who was going to organise the rave for us. We arranged to have it on the Friday night after the Night Owl, so we had three days to organise it. We were so looking forward to catching up with everyone in the Night Owl, getting off our faces, and dancing. We figured with the water and electric situation, we could stick it down there for a few days and then we'd fuck off back home. The next few days, we spread the word around. A few people called to see us because they had heard we were back home; it felt like we had been away for months.

On Thursday, Matt called up with his crew to set everything up; there were transit vans and bodies all over the place. The canteen would be the main area for the DJ and the dance floor, and one of the rooms was designated to serve tea, coffee, pop, water and chewing gum, with another room for the chill-out area. He set up some generators and the DJ area, and a few girls were sorting out the stalls and the chill-out room. They hung tie-dyed sheets on the walls and off the rafters, set up a face-painting area in another room, and even brought in bales of hay for people to sit on. It was a proper job, Matt was on the fucking ball with it all; he'd even arranged all the DJs and said that Danny Slade, the resident DJ of the Night

Owl, would be coming back to the party and playing a set as well. We loved Danny Slade; he played my type of music—hard house. Matt had also made some flyers. Well, not flyers exactly; he used the machine in the services to print business cards.

Friday came and everything was in place. Matt called up with a few people to add some finishing touches and to do a sound test; everything sounded great. We had a smoke machine and strobe lights, and the girls had stocked up their little shop. We were all excited as fuck. The plan was to go down the Night Owl, hand out the flyers and when it finished, lead a convoy to our rave. But then we noticed a police car coming up the drive towards us. It stopped in front of me and Rob, and two coppers jumped out.

One of the coppers said…

"We have reason to believe that you intend to hold an illegal rave on this property; therefore, I have been instructed to inform you to cease all activities, remove any equipment you have set up or installed and leave the premises as you found it."

Now, Matt had already mentioned to us that this might happen and explained exactly what to do if the circumstances arose. He told us to keep our mouths shut and let him do all the talking.

Matt looked over at the copper and said…

"This is a private party, invitation only. We are legally renting the property and the land; therefore, you have no jurisdiction here."

He expected that answer because he just ploughed on with his questions…

"Has the landlord permitted you to hold an illegal rave on this land? Is the landlord aware that you are holding an illegal rave on his property?"

"Yes, the landlord is fully aware and has no objections. In fact, he told us to crack on and have a great private party."

Again he fired his questions at Matt…

"Where is the landlord at the moment.?"

"He's on holiday in the Philippines; he can't be contacted but when I speak to him next, I'll let him know you were asking about him."

"What is the landlord's name?"

"Mick Colgan be his name officer."

The copper turned away from us and spoke into his walkie-talkie; we couldn't work out what he was saying but we heard Mick's name being mentioned. Then he chatted with the other copper for about five minutes while we were all just stood around, hoping they would fuck off soon and leave us to it. Then he turned to Matt and said...

"We can confirm that the details you have provided regarding the property owner are correct, although we are unable to contact him to verify that he is aware of an illegal rave on his land. However, I have been advised to allow you to continue with your so-called private party. We will be putting on extra patrols tonight and keeping a close eye on you lot." Then they jumped back in the car and off they fucked.

We all cheered and jumped up and down as they drove off. It felt like we had won some sort of historic battle, us against the justice system, and we beat the system; we were all buzzing off it. Matt was our hero; he had saved the day. So we carried on making sure everything was working; that there were no health & safety hazards and there was wheelchair access, all the normal stuff. But just as we were all about to leave for the Night Owl, we spotted another car coming up the drive very fast, as if they were being chased or in a hurry to get to us. I recognised who it was as it got closer, and so did Rob; it was Pat, Mick's son. He came to a screeching halt in front of us; I could see his wife and the kids in the car with him as well. I thought he was in danger or something. He threw the door open before the dust even settled, his face was bright red and flushed. He looked over to me and Rob and shouted…

"You fucking pair had better get rid of all this stuff and all these fucking people right now. No fucking way are you having any sort of party on my father's property, private or illegal."

None of us had ever heard him swear before, let alone raise his voice. He was definitely Mick's son.

Matt looked over to me and said….

"What the fuck is happening? Who is he? Do you want me to have a word with him?"

"It's Mick's son. The coppers probably contacted him somehow. We'll sort it out now. Leave this one to us."

I turned to Pat and said….

"Look, Pat, it's okay. The police have been up here and they know all about it. They are even going to put on some extra patrols to make sure it's run safely."

"I couldn't give a fuck if the Pope gave it his personal blessing. You all need to vacate the premises. Please"

"It's okay, Pat. We'll clean up after ourselves and leave the place exactly as it was," Rob said.

"I'm sorry, boys, but my father is still liable if anything happens on this property, including any damage, injuries or even deaths. I'm looking after everything now and I can't risk jeopardising this deal, nor can he. And that is my final word."

I looked over at Pat's wife and the kids in the car; she shook her head at me as if to say, "Please don't argue with him." Rob saw that too, and then we both looked at each other and knew the show was over; we had to concede defeat. So that's what we did. Matt was gutted and so was everyone else; it put a real downer on things. We told Pat to give us a couple of hours, then everything would be packed up and we'd be out of there, but before he left, he said....

"Mind you do now, boys, because the police told me they would be ready to come up here if my negotiations failed." He gave out a bit of a chuckle and off he went.

As we packed everything up we kept apologising to Matt and everyone else, but he said...

"It's a shame but it's all part of the illegal rave scene. Some you win and some you lose. It'll make a great story one day."

But on a brighter note, we had a brilliant time in the Night Owl; everyone was happy to see us and we were delighted to see them. The Chef's special that night was Rhubarb and Custards, and we had two servings each. We missed the smell of Vicks vapour rub, poppers and sweat. Danny Slade played a wicked set of uplifting house. He got the place rocking; it was one of the best nights we had down there. We went to another party afterwards, in a barn, and then went to the services. It was good to be back on the scene and we were going to make up for lost time.

My House, My Rules

When I finally arrived back home, the first thing I did was go and get Rip; he was so excited to see me that a little bit of cum secreted from his cock. I was just as happy to see him as well but I didn't cum in my pants. We went for a long walk up the river and he headed straight for his favourite place so I could chuck him in the water. He stood there waiting for me, wagging his tail. I picked him up and threw him in. We repeated that for ages and then we went up the mountain. I told him all about my adventures down Mick's place and the Philippines. He said I should write a book about it. When we got back to my house, Rob was sitting on the pavement outside with his suitcase. It turned out that he had been evicted. He couldn't even get into his flat as they'd fitted one of those big steel doors to the front. There was a notice on the door that his furniture and all his belongings had been taken to the skip. So, to cut a long story short, he had to move in with me until he could find another gullible landlord to rent him a flat. I gave him three rules:

No blasting the music

No using the tumble dryer to dry soaking wet clothes

If Marcia calls over, lock Rip in the kitchen before letting her in.

He said to me…

"Carl, you can make as many rules as you want but you know me when it comes to rules; I see them as more of a challenge. So, good luck with that one. And besides, I haven't seen Rip shagging Marcia's leg yet; there is no way I'm going to miss that opportunity."

Simon had decided to move to Manchester to be closer to his girlfriend but it was really to keep an eye on her after we planted the seeds of doubt in his head about her playing away. So it was just me and Rob. We planned to become DJs but we needed to buy all the equipment, and we needed to buy a car so we could cart all the equipment about and go raving. We still had some of the money that Rose gave us which, put together, came to £900, so the first thing we did was to buy a car. We bought an old Volvo estate from one of our mates which had three months' tax and six months' MOT, but Rob obviously didn't have a driving licence or insurance. He was banned from driving for three years; he was the only person I knew who'd managed to get banned without even having a license but at least the car was legal. He also applied for an emergency loan from social services due to him being homeless and destitute, and within a few days, he received a giro for £750; out of that money, we bought the following equipment:

2 X Technicks SL120's Mark 2

Peavey Speakers

An Amp

Vestax mixer

Some generic disco lights

Strobe machine

Smoke machine

1 standard microphone

Loads of vinyl

Rob bought hardcore and I bought house.

I won't tell you where we bought the equipment from because I'm not a grass but we bought the records from Spillers record shop in Cardiff. The first vinyl Rob bought was:

Skin Up – A Juicy Red Apple.

And the first vinyl I bought was:

New Atlantic – I Know.

We set everything up in my living room and tested it all out, including how loud the amp and speakers were.

It was the only time I allowed Rob to blast the music as loud as it would go. It wasn't the only time that he blasted the music as loud as it would go but it was the only time I gave him permission to do it. We were very satisfied with the results but the neighbours weren't happy at all, not only in my street; we had complaints from people living two streets over. Plus the house was full of smoke because we didn't know how to turn the smoke machine down. Anyway, we needed to come up with a name for ourselves. Rob chose DJ Tooshay because when he had his dungarees and green bucket hat on, he looked a bit like a turtle (Tooshay turtle for you youngsters out there). I didn't know what to call myself; Rob suggested DJ Smiley because I was always smiling so I went with that. I didn't really like the name but I couldn't think of anything else. We also had a strapline…

"One black, one white, two decks and a mic."

We would practice mixing on the decks all day. I tried to make sure that Rob kept the volume down but he would always secretly turn it up a little bit at a time, hoping I wouldn't notice, and if ever I needed to go out or pop to the shop, he would blast it. We had so many arguments over it; they would usually go something like this…

"Rob, the music is loud enough as it is; you don't need to turn it up. Why do you do it when you know I've told you not to?"

"It's because you told me not to. I just can't help it."

"So if I told you to turn the music up when I leave the house, would you turn it down?"

"No, I'd listen to you then."

"So what do I need to say for you not to turn the music up?"

"There's nothing you can say, Carl. If I were you, I'd stop wasting my breath."

"At least have some respect for Gladys next door."

"I do. I put a bit of Tom Jones on for her. She told me she likes Tom Jones."

"For fucks sake, Rob mun; I can't wait for you to get a flat and move out. And what have I told you about putting soaking wet clothes in the tumble dryer?"

"I remember exactly what you said, Carl. You told me not to do it because it eats the electric."

"Well, why do you do it then?"

"You're not paying the electricity bill, Carl. So why do you care.?"

"Because one day I might have to pay it and all the arrears as well. So the less I have to pay back, the better."

"The problem with you, Carl, is you worry too much about things that might never happen. It's no good for your head; it'll fuck you up in the end, just concentrate on the now."

"Yeah, and the problem with you is that you don't worry enough about anything."

"I don't have a problem with that, Carl. It seems to me that you've got a problem with me not having a problem."

He ended up staying with me for about a month. Neither of us really enjoyed the experience and we vowed never to live together again. He got a flat on the local housing estate and took all the equipment with him. I felt pity for his neighbours. Not long after that, we started getting bookings to do discos but Rob only wanted to play hardcore, and we were being booked to do birthday parties and weddings. We had lots of arguments over that as well. I ended up buying a load of rave/pop crossover records to play. Rob did buy one non-rave record; it was:

Michael Bolton – How Am I Supposed to Live Without You.

He said we could play that for the slow dance at weddings. For some reason, he loved that song. I'd often pop over to his flat and hear it blasting out of his windows as I turned the corner onto his estate. Most of our bookings were for teenagers' birthday parties because they had all heard of raves but had never been to one; they wanted to hear proper hardcore instead of the chart music and Rob was more than happy to blast it into their eardrums as loud as he could. It was good because their parties were mainly on weeknights, but we didn't start work until a Thursday so any birthday parties or discos would have to be a Thursday night. That meant that our weekends would begin on a Thursday as well because after the Philippines we got the taste for alcohol again and would get drunk as we were doing the discos; we would never drink if we went to a rave though. So, we never really made much money from discos because we would spend most of our earnings behind the bar. When Rob was on the decks, I would dance on the stage, and when it was my turn on the decks, he would dance and do a bit of MCing as well. But his vocabulary on the Mic was very limited. His repertoire went something like this:

You know the score fucking hardcore.
Come on, all you motherfuckers out there

241

let me see you move.

Easygroove, Easygroove, Easygroove

We even had two of our mates come with us as dancers; they would dress up in boiler suits and face masks and dance on the stage. They called themselves "Bill & Ben, The XTC Men"; you could never get away with that now. We were booked for a wedding once and Rob played hardcore all night; he wouldn't let me go on the decks and they all complained about it afterwards. Luckily, we had cash up front and he did play Michael Bolton for them as the last song.

We would also DJ in the local pubs, hire a hall in the Welfare Club, and hold rave nights on Saturdays, charging at the door to make money for beer. We always had a few people to help us out and man the door for us while we were busy pretending to be rave DJs; then afterwards we would have parties back at my house. One Sunday afternoon, we were all chilling out in my living room when one of my neighbours knocked on the door; the conversation went like this...

"Alright, Carl. Now, you know me, I don't mind what you get up to; it's none of my business. I was young once, believe it or not, and I could tell you some stories."

"Alright, Ron. You want to relive your youth, do you?"

"No, of course not. I'm just here to warn you that a petition is going around the street to get you evicted. I've even signed it myself because I wouldn't hear the end of it from the wife if I didn't, and officially, I'm here to tell you to keep the noise down, but I also wanted to tell you about the petition."

"Oh right, thanks for letting me know, Ron; I might sign it myself."

"Well, I thought I'd better tell you, but as far as I'm concerned, you lot are just doing what youngsters should be doing and enjoying your lives because before you know it, you'll have arthritis in your knees, and you'll be back and forth to the toilet all night pissing."

"I appreciate it, Ron; thanks for the heads up."

And off he went.

I knew they couldn't evict me because it was a private house so I wasn't worried about it. If it had been a council house, it would have been a different matter altogether.

I'm not sure how it happened but somehow I got addicted to Marathon chocolate bars; they are called Snickers now, but for the purpose of this book, I will still call them "Marathons" because that's what they were called at the time. I would eat as many of them as I could get my hands on; I'm talking about ten or fifteen of them a day, if not more. I think it must have been the sugar content or the salt because I wasn't really eating properly back then as I didn't have a lot of money to buy food. I'd get what I could for me and Rip but I would never be able to afford to do a food shop once a week or even once a month.

Anyway, I'd be back and forth to the shop all day buying Marathons and whenever anyone called down to my house, the rule was they had to bring a Marathon with them to gain entry; if they didn't have one, I'd send them over the shop to get one before I let them in. I even stuck an empty wrapper above my door to remind people and for some reason, I kept all the empty packets. I would store them in the drawers, cupboards, and underneath the cushions. I remember my older brother called down to the house one day. He opened the cupboard to get a glass and it was full of empty Marathon wrappers. He already thought I was losing the plot and that sealed it for him. Even the kids in the street started posting empty wrappers through my letter box and I also devised a little game for when people came to my house. I hid ten empty Marathon wrappers in the living room in ornaments, behind pictures, or out of plain sight, and they would have to find them all. There was no prize but it was a good laugh and something fun to do with the new people who came back to my house.

Rob called to my house one day, more animated and excited than usual. He said…

"Come outside and look at what I got for us."

"What is it?"

"Well, come outside and I'll show you."

I got up and followed him outside. Parked in front of my house was a beach buggy. A bright, fluorescent, sparkly pink beach buggy, to be precise.

"Is that yours?"

"It's ours, Carl; we've gone halfers on it."

"What do you mean we've gone halfers? Who did you buy it from? How much?"

"That's the beauty of it, Carl, it won't cost us fuck all."

"What the fuck are you on about, Rob? How can we go halfers but it won't cost us fuck all?"

"I had it off Barry, who runs the Woolpack. He said we could have it as long as we do some discos in his pub, and we can play hardcore. He's trying to get a rave night going and if it kicks off, he'll pay us to do more."

It was shaped like a Volkswagen Beetle but with the roof cut off. The body was fibreglass and there was no windscreen or doors. Obviously, it had no Tax or MOT, but it did have a licence plate on it, so it was roadworthy to a degree.

"Jump in, I'll take you for a spin. You'll have to give me a bump start though."

"Why do you need a bump start?"

"The starter motor is fucked but we can get that fixed."

So I gave him a push and off we went up to the river because he wanted to show me what it was like on rough terrain. It wasn't very comfortable, I know that much, and I kept sliding over to the driver's side all the time. It did have seat belts though; that was the one good thing. He was driving up and down the grass verges, through the mud, and into all the big puddles. I wasn't really enjoying his daredevil manoeuvres; he was driving it as if it were a dump truck. Then we went through a puddle, hit a big stone in the middle, and heard a loud splitting noise. We got out of the buggy to have a look at what had happened and that's when I noticed rainbows appearing in the puddle and then a trail of petrol coming from the puddle to the buggy. On closer inspection, we noted that he had cracked the petrol tank open so we had to push it back to my house. There was no way we could replace the tank because it was part of the buggy, and we didn't know how to get a fibreglass petrol tank repaired. But as luck would have it, my stepfather had an old mini in the garden that he was "doing up". He hadn't done fuck all with it for months, it would probably end up rusting away, and the scrap man would take it like the rest of the cars he always meant to fix. So we took the petrol tank off the mini. It wouldn't fit underneath the buggy but it fit on the back seat. We managed to divert the pipes from the original petrol tank from the engine to the mini petrol tank in the back; it wedged in nicely as well. It was tight as fuck back there but it didn't move about, that's for sure.

For the next few weeks, we drove everywhere in the beach buggy. We just had to be careful in petrol stations and make sure the attendant didn't see us pumping the petrol into a tank sitting on the back seat. Of course, if anyone was sat in the back, they weren't allowed to smoke. We even drove down to the Night Owl in Tenby. That was brilliant, especially for the beach party after-wards; Rob was taking everyone for a spin around the beach. We didn't enjoy the drive home, though. That 50 miles felt like we were driving in a blizzard; we had no protection from the wind or other elements. We went down to Swansea one day to see our friend Lisa and take her to the beach. I always remember the look on her face when she saw the buggy and then spotted the petrol tank in the back seat. She looked over at us and said:

"What's that doing there? Is it the actual petrol tank?"

"Yes, it's alright, though; it's safe. Just don't smoke next to it."

"I'm not jumping in the back next to that. It's dangerous."

"It's alright, mun. It won't move; it's solid."

"No way. Sorry boys but, as well as dangerous, it's illegal."

"I'll jump in the back, you jump in the front," I told her.

She was a bit reluctant but Rob convinced her it was safe and wouldn't catch fire or anything like that.

She eventually agreed to come with us as long as I sat in the back.

In the end, Rob was caught driving around the village, the police seized it from him, and he was banned from driving for another eighteen months.

RIP, Rip

One Saturday afternoon, a few of us were in my house when there was a knock on the door from one of my neighbours. I thought he was going to complain about something but instead, he said...

"Your dog has been run over on the main road."

"My dog?"

"Yes, your Airedale terrier, he's been run over."

"Where?"

"On the main road"

"You sure it's my dog?"

"Yes. Scruffy little black thing. I saw a car hit him."

The others in the house heard him and we ran up the main road, my neighbour following. We couldn't see anything. Rip wasn't lying on the side of the road, dead or alive; he wasn't anywhere to be seen.

My neighbour stood beside me and said...

"The car must have taken his body. Either that or he's in them bushes."

He pointed to some stinging nettles behind the bus stop. We all searched them, not caring if they hurt, but none of us could find him. We searched all over the place; a few of my mates jumped in their car and searched further up the road as well but they couldn't see any trace of him either.

"Are you sure it was my dog?" I asked my neighbour.

"It was definitely your dog."

We searched for hours, walking along both sides of the road for about three miles, but we couldn't find him. I was hoping that my neighbour was wrong. We went back to the house, the mood really sombre. We all burst into tears as soon as we were all assembled in my living room. Everyone knew Rip and they got on well with him; he was part of my house, part of the furniture, and part of me. The next day, we all looked for him again, retracing our steps just in case we missed something, but we still couldn't find him. In a way, I was glad we didn't find his body because secretly, I could kid myself that he just ran off because he'd had enough of living with me and was shacking up with another family. I needed some closure, so we all decided to have a little funeral in the back garden for him. One of the girls made a little cross, we bought flowers, and I wrote a poem. I put it on the next page so it all stays intact…

R.I.P

Rip has gone, he's left me alone,

There's no more Rip, he's not coming home

I let him out last night like I usually do

But when I got back there was no Ripper Roo.

I went out the back to give him a shout

I called his name but he wasn't about

I thought nothing of it and shouted no more

The very next day there was a knock on the door.

I answered the door and it was a friend

He told me Rip's life had come to an end

He'd been run over on the main road

I couldn't believe what I was told.

We looked for Rip that very same day

We searched the place where he last lay

Nowhere to be found was the dog from number seven

So Ripper Roo must now be in heaven.

His death hit me really hard. He had been our family dog; my mother's dog. He was part of the character of the house and it would never be the same without him; neither would I. Anyway, enough of that; I actually cried while I was writing it.

251

Raving Mad

As well as doing discos, we still went to as many raves as possible. Raving always took priority over everything else; we'd even turn down bookings if it meant we would have to miss a rave. But it also meant that we would get little or no sleep at all every weekend as we even did some discos on a Sunday night. We weren't eating properly either; I was down to about eight and a half stone when I should have been around ten.

Our nearest local rave club was "Martha's Vineyard" in Swansea, known simply as "Martha's"; it was hardcore as fuck in there. The music was hardcore, the people were hardcore, and the atmosphere was hardcore. It was run by the Tick Tock crew I mentioned earlier. DJ Lomas, one of the resident DJs, was like our Welsh version of Easygroove. Then you had Jammo and Jez, who knew exactly what we wanted to hear and had the perfect tracks to keep us stomping.

The Swansea crew were all nuts, it was like a mental hospital in there; no normal conversations ever took place among us and that's how I liked it. The party vibe hit you the second you walked through the doors; everyone was drenched in sweat, shaking hands and hugging each other as they danced. The main floor downstairs

252

held the rawest energy; it was intense. I mentioned earlier about the guy in Pulse with the "Radeon" t-shirt. Well, he was one of the Martha's crew, he would set the mood on the dance floor, and the mood was always hardcore; he knew the score. Rob would often dance by the side of him, both complimenting each other through their love of hardcore stomping. There was an upstairs area as well and it was the only place I had ever been to where the stairs felt like another room. People would spend hours sitting on the stairs, chatting to each other or chatting to those going up or down. I often sat on the stairs talking utter bollocks to some fucker or just hung around there so I could meet and greet people as they were passing. Upstairs was a bit more chilled out and relaxed, where the off-it people hung about. I met some right headers in that place and made some good friends, so a big shout out to all the Martha's crew and the Tick Tock crew. You know the score. Fucking hardcore.

We also went to a good few illegal raves in mansions, warehouses, fields, barns, a disused railway tunnel, and empty car parks. I loved being in a convoy, evading the police, and eventually finding the place; it was all part of the thrill. We went to one rave in a warehouse that was busted by the police. Within about an hour, we were all congregated in a field, back on it and back at it. Then afterwards, it was off to the services. I had so much fun in the services; it was like another playground to me. I would walk around talking utter shit to people, we would all talk shit to each other, everyone had mega vivid imaginations, and we would sit and talk for hours about the price of a tin of beans, or we'd read each other's tea leaves or make up a song. I'd meet up with someone I danced with earlier and we'd chat; they would be just as crazy to chat with as they were on the dance floor. There was one time that about two hundred of us descended on a services at about four o'clock in the morning. Me and Rob sat down, and he just started giggling and couldn't stop; everyone else started noticing it and looking at him. He was wearing a Troop tracksuit at the time, and someone shouted out:

"Troops got the giggles, Troops got the giggles."

And then everyone started chanting it over and over."

"Troops got the giggles. Troops got the giggles. Troops got the giggles. Troops got the giggles…"

It was trippy as fuck. Two hundred people chanting it at Rob; it spun him right out. He got up off his chair and darted to the exit, while everyone burst out laughing. He was gone for about two minutes and I thought he was having a downer; it would have spun the fuck out of me but he came back a few minutes later, laughing his head off, and everyone laughed with him. It was a surreal experience.

We even managed to organise our very own illegal rave in an industrial unit we rented out. We hired a place on an industrial estate in Swansea, telling the landlord we were musicians and only wanted to hire it for a week as a music studio. He wanted us to rent it for a month minimum so we explained that as soon as we'd recorded the song we were working on, we'd be touring the country promoting it, but when we got back, we would hire it for longer to record our album. We figured that by telling him we were using it as a recording studio, if he had any complaints about loud music, he would explain that we were musicians recording a song; it was Rob's idea to tell him that, which I thought was very cunning of him. We gave him false names and a false address, and paid him cash up front. We had also parked the car on another part of the estate when we met him outside the unit. We told him we got lost driving around the industrial estate so decided it was easier to park and find it on foot. That was my idea, in case he wrote our licence plate number down; I was always paranoid when it came to doing anything dodgy.

Rob was going to be on the decks all night playing his hardcore and I said I might play a bit of hard house if

255

I felt comfortable enough. Rob didn't give a fuck that he couldn't mix properly and he didn't know how to match the BPM. Neither did I, but I didn't want to make a fool of myself; that was another thing Rob cared fuck-all about. We hired the unit on a Monday and planned to have the rave on the Friday after the Night Owl. That would give us enough time to get all the equipment down there and sort out any other shit we needed. By Thursday, all of our equipment was in place and we tested it to make sure everything was working. We even had a few of the girls set up a little stall selling tea, coffee, water and chewing gum. We went to the services and used the machine to print business cards as flyers, like the ones Matt made for us for the rave that never was. The meeting point was in Penllergaer Services at two o'clock, after the Night Owl finished.

Friday night arrived as it always does; a gang of us went down the Night Owl, we handed out the flyers, and just before it closed, the girls and a few of the boys headed back to the unit to man the doors, put the kettle on, and wait for people to arrive. Meanwhile, me and Rob headed to the services, getting there just before two o'clock, and waited for people to arrive. Arrive they did and off we set, telling everyone to follow us. We were the lead car in a convoy, which was a hell of a buzz. I kept looking back every time we turned a corner to watch everyone follow us. There were about thirty vehicles in our convoy and we were hyped up to fuck; that was one of my favourite memories of the rave scene. When we reached the warehouse, we could hear music playing; someone was on the decks. We recognised who it was once we got inside; MC Digger and his crew from Cardiff. They ended up playing on the decks all night; Rob never got a chance but he didn't mind because it meant he could dance all night and get off it. I didn't mind because it was less stress for me but I still couldn't really relax for some reason, so I served tea and coffee and went on the door, letting people in; altogether, throughout the night, about a hundred and fifty people turned up. As I was on the door, I spotted some plain clothes coppers get out of a car; they were easy to spot because they looked straight as fuck and were wearing clothes you would wear to a nightclub. Three of them walked towards me to enter the building. I put my hand out to stop them and said:

"Invite only, sorry."

"Whose party is it then?"

"You won't know him, mate; he's not from around here."

"How do we get an invite?"

"If you haven't had one already, then you haven't been invited. Sorry, officer."

"Did you organise the party?"

"No comment"

At the same time as I was talking to them, I was letting other people pass me without showing an invite.

"How come they don't need an invite then?" he said to me.

"No comment"

"Okay, we understand. We'll just keep an eye on everyone from the car."

And off they went to keep an eye on everyone. Mind you, they did look a bit menacing, but they didn't deter us. The rave finished at about nine o'clock in the morning. We cleaned the place up as best we could, posted the keys through the letterbox, and a gang of us went back to my house. All in all, it was a great success and even though I didn't really enjoy it myself, everyone else did.

On the subject of the Night Owl, one Friday afternoon me and Rob were sitting in my house, skint as fuck, trying to work out a way how to get down there. Rob had a car but we didn't even have enough money for petrol, let alone refreshments. As luck would have it, one of our old friends popped in to see us. He was desperate to offload some contraband he had acquired; a black bag full of cigarettes that had fallen out of a vending machine in a pub. Two hundred packets, to be exact, containing a total of 3,600 cigarettes. He was very keen to turn them into cash but we didn't have any cash on us, so we came to a "buy now, pay later" arrangement, otherwise known as a "lay on." So the plan was to sell some in the car park when we got down the Night Owl and then sell the rest of them inside to make enough money for refreshments. But we still needed petrol money to get down there, so we went door to door in my street selling them until we'd made enough, then off we went.

Now, around the time of the raves down the Night Owl, there was a lot of bad publicity going on concerning ravers, and there was talk of the Criminal Justice Bill (CJB) coming into power to stop people gathering and dancing to "repetitive beats." So every now and then, the police would set up roadblocks or "Stop Checks" to search vehicles for drugs. I remember one time the police were on a roundabout. We were all in a massive convoy and they blocked the exit of the road we were all heading for, forcing us to split up; then they sent us all off in different directions. At each roundabout, they were diverting a load of us down one exit, then blocking it off and diverting another load to a different exit. Anyway, as we were heading towards the Tenby road, I could see traffic slowing up ahead of us, and then I spotted the police vans and cars parked on the banking. There was no way we could turn around because the traffic was already forming a queue behind us, so we slowed down. There was a big queue ahead of us, about thirty or forty vehicles. The police were letting most of the cars through but we could see they had pulled some of them over and were searching them at the side of the road. As we got closer, one of the coppers spotted us and signalled Rob to pull over. He then told him to turn the engine off and instructed us to wait in the car for the search team. There were about three cars in front of us that they had pulled over, all full of ravers. We watched as the police searched the vehicles and everyone in them, then bundled some people into the back of the police van.

I was panicking like fuck. All I was thinking about was the stolen cigarettes in the boot; it was obvious they were from a vending machine because there were only 18 cigarettes in each packet, and the seal around them said "Vending Machine." The biggest giveaway was that they were in the boot of our car and not in a vending machine and although we didn't steal them ourselves, they would have us on suspicion of handling stolen goods or something like that. That meant, at the very least, they would keep us in the cells overnight. We didn't have anything else on us so we weren't worried about that. Rob wasn't concerned about anything. I turned to him and said.

"What are we gonna do? What are we gonna say?"

"Don't worry about it, Carl. I'll do all the talking; you just keep your mouth shut and stop looking so fucking guilty, will you?"

"Well, we are fucking guilty; guilty of handling stolen goods. We've got over three thousand stolen goods in the boot, Rob."

"They can't prove they're stolen, Carl. I'll tell them we've been working for my uncle, demolishing a pub, and they were left in the basement. He'll back us up if they have to phone him. We might have to spend a few hours in the police station but we'll be down the Night Owl in time for Colin Dale's set. Don't worry about it."

"What if they ask you about your driving licence?"

"I'll give my brother's name; I always do. They'll ask me to produce my documents at the police station in a few days, I'll take his documents down and pretend to be him. They never check that type of stuff."

"Well, at least the car has tax and an MOT."

"Well, the MOT ran out last week but I can get a dodgy one to produce. But you're right about the tax disc."

They had finished searching the car in front of us and we were next. Just as the copper approached us with the search team, his radio went off. He stopped and spoke into his walkie-talkie, then chatted with the search team; then he came to the window and said:

"It's your lucky day, boys. We've been called out to an incident in Saundersfoot, so you're free to go."

And off he went.

And off we went.

As we were driving away, Rob looked at me and said:

"See Carl, I told you not to panic; I had it all under control."

"Rob, we just got lucky, that's all."

"Carl, luck is always on my side and if you stick with me, it might rub off on you."

We had a wicked time down the Night Owl. A few key players were missing though, because they'd been caught with drugs on them and detained for the night.

As well as all the local clubs and the illegal raves we went to, we tried to go to as many big raves as possible. We went to every Fantazia event that year:

Second Sight in Exeter

Takes You Into Summertime in Bournemouth

One Step Beyond in Donnington Park

The Showcase in Shepton Mallet

New Year's Eve in Hungerford.

One of my favourite raves ever was "Takes You Into Summertime" in Bournemouth. It was a beautiful sunny day and it really did feel like summer. A gang of us went up in a van and, a few miles before we got to Bournemouth, there were traffic jams full of ravers; we got out of the van and chatted with a few of them. Someone told us that the organisers of Fantazia only had a licence for 8,000 people but had sold 16,000 tickets, so the roads going into Bournemouth were chaos. In the end, they all just parked their cars on the side of the road and the side streets or in front of people's houses, and walked the rest of the way. We managed to get about half a mile from the rave before doing the same. We didn't know where we were going; just followed other ravers through the streets. All the local residents were out and the neighborhood watch was on high alert; it must have looked like some sort of zombie apocalypse to them.

When we eventually arrived at the venue there was a massive queue. They were also allowing people to pay at the gates. Rob managed to sneak in the stage door by walking in with a gang of roadies and dancers. Nobody asked him for a pass and he got in there before all of us. Apparently, there were about twenty thousand of us in there that night, all off our chops in all sorts of weird and wonderful ways; the whole place was bonkers. It was like one big fuck off fun fair ride all night long; I had never seen or been in the company of so many "off it" people in my life. I loved it; I was in my element and played my part on the funny farm. The one other outstanding thing I remember about that rave was what we came to call:

"The Fantazia Theme Tune."

I remember one time I was fucked. It was about five o'clock in the morning and I was lying on the grass. I needed a break; I'd been dancing nonstop for about eight hours and there were loads of others in the same state. Then the DJ played:

DJ Edge – Compnded.

And *everybody* got up to dance. We were all smiling at each other, then we went ballistic; it was pure energy and took the place to a whole new level. It was like a different rave altogether. We danced until the sun came up, then danced some more. I get goosebumps thinking about it. In the morning, when all the music had stopped and it was chucking out time, the MC came on stage and said...

"When you leave, please don't go anywhere near Bournemouth beach; please just go home."

He said that quite a lot and for a while.

I don't know if he was telling people not to go to the beach or letting everyone know there was a party on the beach. Either way, thousands of people descended onto Bournemouth beach afterwards. I didn't go because I was absolutely fucked, and a lot of the others that were with us were in no fit state, so we went home and left Rob to it. He went to the beach with a few people he met in the car park and came home about two days later. I have to admit I was a bit gutted I didn't stay because it sounded wicked.

The other Fantazia that I really enjoyed was in Donnington Park. There was a different type of atmosphere in that one; it was intense but a good kind of intense. I remember walking around in between the crowds and everyone was squeezing each other's shoulders as they passed one another, giving each other little rushes, pulling faces, and nodding at each other. I hugged so many people as I walked among them; we all did. There was that look or glance we would give each other, and you just knew you had to connect physically and squeeze each other; it was really intense. Rob managed to get in free because he helped the security at the gates with a boy who was having a downer; Rob brought him out of it and promised them if they let him in, he would help others inside going through the same. He also climbed onto the top of a set of speakers on the scaffolding when Rat Pack played but the MC told him to get down off the speakers. So then he joined them on stage; they played a wicked set:

I can feel another rush coming on.
Feel it in my body all night long.
Now I was standing in the corner.
I'm searching for my Rizla
I had some marijuana
I needed to get higher.

Fantazia was also our first big New Year's Eve rave. It was in Littlecote House near Newbury so it wasn't far for us. The flyer said it was in a "16th-century mansion" but it was in big marquees *near* a mansion. The only thing I remember about that rave was that it was freezing and very muddy, and in the morning, in the car park, it was chaos because we were instructed to park in the fields and everyone was struggling to get their cars out because it was a mud bath.

We also went to a lot of the other big raves as well, such as:

Dreamscape

Perception

Obsession

Exodus

Dance Planet

Vision

Amnesia House

Universe

I had the same ritual in every rave; as soon as I got inside, I would fuck off on my own and find the toilets. I always had butterflies in my stomach and I'd be excited as fuck so I needed to off load. Then, if there was a fun-fair, I would go on the waltzers; I liked being spun around because it brought me up. After that I would find the gar-age tent, which would be my base for the night.

We would also take things with us as props to use in the car park or services afterwards, to cheer people up or just to fuck about and have a laugh because the rave scene was all about characters. We met a lot of crazy characters and wanted to play our part in the circus. We bought two glove puppets and Rob named his "Bill", while I named mine "Not Bill"; I think they were little squirrels. We would take them into the chill-out room and try to cheer people up and help them if they were on a downer. We would only talk to them through our puppets, which some loved, and it did bring them out of their downers. But we scared the fuck out of a few people; it really tripped them out, especially with our strong Welsh accents.

I would also take a children's storybook with me called *The House That Jack Built*. You may have heard of it; it goes like this…

This is the house that Jack built.
This is the malt that lay in the house that Jack built.
This is the rat that ate the malt
That lay in the house that Jack built.
This is the cat
That killed the rat that ate the malt
That lay in the house that Jack built.

It was much longer than that but only about a five-minute read. I would walk around the car park in the mornings, looking for people sitting in their cars, and if I spotted an empty seat in the car, I would ask them if I

268

could sit inside and read them a story. Most people said yes. I would also take a box of cornflakes and a bowl. I would fill the bowl up with cornflakes and walk around asking if anyone had any milk for my cornflakes. Rob would wear his slippers to raves because he said they were more comfortable and easier to dance in. It earned him the nickname "Slippers." He also carried around a little teddy bear called "Snootsie", introducing it to everyone he met, and adding a playful charm to his already memorable presence.

A friend of ours introduced us to the poem *Desiderata*, by Max Ehrmann. We loved it and thought everyone should live by its words. After we read it, we decided that it would be our way of life, so we printed it out, and the both of us would walk around the car park reciting it to people:

"Go placidly amid the noise and the haste and remember what peace there may be in silence. As far as possible, without surrender, be on good terms with all persons."

I don't think I can write the whole poem but if you haven't read it, look it up. It really is something we should all aspire to replicate in our lives.

One of the weirdest raves I went to was Amnesia House – The Wedding. I did enjoy it, but there was an atmosphere in there that I had never felt before in a rave. It was a kind of disconnection; it didn't feel like we were all together as one and I'd never felt that in a rave before. It was in Northamptonshire, which was about 177.2 miles away from my house. We took a load of people up with us. It was billed as the first-ever wedding ceremony in a rave. Micky Lynas, one of the organisers of Amnesia House, was going to get married live on stage in front of 15,000 ravers, and Grooverider was his best man. There was a good line-up there as well: The Prodigy, Top Buzz, Jumping Jack Frost, Mickey Finn. The flyer also said there would be a surprise P.A. and the rumour was that it was KLF. We didn't care much about the wedding but thought it would be good to be part of history in the making.

We left early in the afternoon and ended up getting lost; we were near Northampton but nowhere near the rave. One of the boys spotted a small sign on a lamp post that said "Michael & Sophie's Wedding." Now, we knew the guy getting married was called Mick so, even though we didn't know the name of the bride, we assumed Michael was his full name and we followed the sign. There were a few more of them on lampposts leading us down some back lanes and winding roads, which we thought was promising because it was out of the way. Then we came to a little church with a bride and groom outside having their pictures taken with the wedding guests, and that's when we realised we'd followed the signs to the wrong wedding. They were the only people we had seen for miles so we all got out of the van and asked them if they knew where Brayfield Stadium was. Nobody knew because they weren't from the area, but we did end up having a picture with the bride and groom because they thought it was funny when we told them how we were looking for a rave and followed their signs.

Anyway, we eventually managed to find the rave. The car park was ram-packed and the queue to get in stretched for miles; it was the longest queue I had ever been in for a rave, in terms of both distance and time. It took about two and a half hours to get through the gates and people were coming up and down off their pills while just waiting to get in. Rob found a ticket on the floor; he went around asking loads of people if they had lost a ticket but they all said no, so he used it himself to get in.

When I got inside, the atmosphere was weird. It was the first time I felt disconnected from everyone in a rave. People were a bit standoffish and not as friendly as I was used to. When the wedding came on, the music stopped and we couldn't really hear what they were saying on the stage. I suppose, on paper, it sounded like a good idea, but in actual practice, it brought the mood down even more because we all just wanted to dance. But although it was a strange rave, I enjoyed it. In the early hours of the morning, I needed a break from dancing and walked around meeting people, deciding I wanted to gather twelve disciples together; fuck knows why. So I went around asking people if they wanted to be my disciples and managed to gather all twelve; they walked around with me as I recited Desiderata to everyone. I also told people that it was my garden and they were all disturbing my peace, and I told them to talk quietly and clean up after themselves. But yes, the wedding certainly was a bit strange.

If you were to ask me what rave events were my favourite to go to, hands down I would have to say it was the "Universe" raves. I loved the whole set-up and vibe about them; they felt more like a festival than a rave. The first Universe we went to was called "Pleasure Planet"; it was also the first ever big outdoor organised rave in Wales and only down the road from us, in Newport. When we saw the flyer we couldn't believe it; a big rave on our doorstep for a change, so obviously loads more people from the village came with us. There was a bouncy castle and a fun fair.

The garage tent was called "The Erogenous Zone", where Nick Warren played the best set of the night, in my opinion; that was the night I fell in love with "Hard House." There was a PA system outside from a crew called "DIY Sound System", and it was playing the funkiest house music I had ever heard; it was like a revelation. There was something I was missing in raves; I didn't know what it was or that it was even missing, but when I heard that music I knew somehow I was longing for it and after that rave, you would always find me in the garage tent at parties. It brought out a completely different set of dance moves in me. That was when I started to dance properly instead of stomping. My body needed more rhythm to express itself; house music provided it and I lapped it up.

I remember the exact moment it hit me, too. I was walking out of the hardcore tent and the PA system outside was playing…

Raze – Break 4 Love.

And then he mixed in…

K-Klass – Rhythm is a Mystery.

I stayed outside all night and, after that, I was in my element. We went to all the Universe raves. In fact, the last big outdoor rave I went to was a Universe.

Blodwen

In October 1992, I met Blodwen. I already knew of her but we had never spoken to each other. She was five years older than me; I was twenty at the time, and she was twenty-five. Me and Rob were doing a disco in the local rugby club. I went to the bar to get a drink and she was standing next to me waiting to be served. She accused me of leading her cousin astray, getting him into drugs and taking him to raves. I knew who her cousin was and told her I didn't make anybody take drugs, which was very true, but I did take him to his first rave; what he did when he got inside was not down to me. I could also see that although she was serious, she wanted to talk more, so we had a bit of banter by the bar.

At the end of the night, I walked her home and we had a little kiss. After that night, whenever we saw each other out we would flirt, and a few weeks later we started courting. I had never had a proper girlfriend before so it was all very new to me and I didn't really know how to be a proper boyfriend; I was still very childish and she was so grown up and straight. She had her own house and an eight-year-old daughter called Sam from a previous marriage; I had no job, no prospects, no responsibilities, and no idea what the future held for me. I wasn't really boyfriend material in my head but we really got on and I liked her a lot, and it was obvious she liked me too. I would call down to her house on weeknights after she put Sam to bed and she would always cook me a meal because I still wasn't eating properly; I was down to about seven and a half stone by that time. She always had coal for her fire as well so it was lovely and warm as we watched TV and talked all night. I never slept there in the beginning and I would always go home at about one o'clock in the morning. She had a full-time job as well and wasn't into raving or anything like that. Like I said, she was quite straight and properly grown up and responsible, unlike me.

After a couple of months, Blodwen told her daughter about us so after that, I could stay for the night. I didn't see much of her on weekends though, because I was busy raving. She did come to a few of our local gigs but I would stay out partying afterwards, while she went home. Then on a Monday, I would call down to her house and stay the night. In the morning, when she got up for work and took her daughter to school, I would stay in bed, waiting for *Neighbours* to come on. I even thought of getting a job and calming down a bit with the raving. I wanted to spend more time with Blodwen and do things on the weekend with her like a proper family, and take her daughter to a zoo or a fun fair. But I didn't have any money and I couldn't drive, and Blodwen was spending extra money on food for me as well, so I felt a bit crap about that and about my situation.

On my twenty-first birthday, she really spoiled me; she bought me a watch because she said my timekeeping was shit, plus a nice thick warm winter jacket, a woolly hat, scarf and gloves because she said I always looked cold. She was right; I've always been a bit of a freezer and the first thing I would do when I went to her house was sit in front of the coal fire. She took me out for a meal with Sam too; I had never been to a proper restaurant before. When we got back to her house, she had even made me a little birthday cake, with candles as well, and they both sang happy birthday to me. I cried; I always get sentimental on my birthday because of my mother.

Christmas came, and it was one of the best I'd had in a few years. I went over to Blodwen's in the morning to watch Sam opening her presents. I enjoyed it and got on well with Sam; she thought I was funny. I didn't buy anything for them because I was skint but I got them a card and wrote a poem for them. Blodwen bought me loads of socks, some jumpers and a pair of trainers; all the things I desperately needed. We went over to her parents' house for Christmas dinner and then we spent the night together. Rob wanted me to do a disco with him but for the first time ever, I declined because I was enjoying spending time with Blodwen. Sometimes, I would take him down to her house with me; I told her that if you have me as a boyfriend, Rob would always be around somewhere, or if he wasn't around, he would be on his way. Rob got on with Blodwen and could see that she was good for me, even though sometimes he would be pissed off that I was spending a lot less time with him.

What Goes up Must Come Down

On Tuesday, 2nd February 1993, it all came crashing down on me. Me and Rob had been to a friend's house in Swansea and as he was driving us home, we were about to turn into my street and I noticed a load of police cars outside my house, along with a van from the electricity board; all my neighbours were out as well. He stopped the car at the bottom of the road and I ducked down. We had a good view of what was going on and watched as the police broke my door down with a battering ram, then some guy from the electricity board entered my house, along with a few coppers. I didn't bother making my presence known.

I didn't have the head on me to deal with it and there was nothing I could say or do to change the situation anyway; I might even have been arrested. It was obvious what had happened; the electricity board needed to gain entry to my house to cut the electric supply off and they brought reinforcements in case of any trouble. So I went down to Blodwen's house and told her all about my dilemma. She said she would borrow money from her father to pay the bill but I said no to that idea. I knew what I had to do but I needed a night to sleep on it.

The following morning, I decided to go to my stepfather's house and explain what had happened, although he'd probably already heard because gossip like that travels quickly around the village. Before I went to see him, I called to my house to evaluate the damage but as I walked in the house he was sitting in the living room with my older brother. They both went ape shit on me, and rightly so; I had fucked up big time. I had no defence to give them so I just kept apologising and telling them I would sort it out.

The mad thing about it all was that both of them had argued with their girlfriends and had been chucked out the night before; they had been looking for me everywhere so it was a good thing they didn't know where Blodwen lived. They spent the night in the house without power as the electricity board had removed the whole box and taken it with them; the timing of it was fucking ironic. My stepfather told me he had already spoken to them on the phone; they wanted £100 up front to put the box back in, then they would fit a meter so the rest of the money could be paid off through electricity tokens. The way it worked was if I bought a £5 electric token, £1 of it would go straight to the electricity board to pay off the arrears and I'd have £4 worth of electricity. I told my stepfather I would sort out the £100; meanwhile, he had already phoned one of his mates to fit a new door.

I wasn't sure where to get the money from but then I had an idea. I asked one of my friends if he could get me a loan from the Provident woman, and I would pay him back weekly; I couldn't go to her directly because she had refused me previously. I didn't pass her credit checks, whatever they were. He got the loan the same day and I gave the money to my stepfather. He contacted the electricity board to pay them and they told him it would take three working days to get around to fitting the new box.

I decided to stay at Blodwen's house for three days but unfortunately, my stepfather and brother had to stay in the house without electricity. I couldn't help but laugh to myself when I called in one night and they were both sitting in the living room with candles on the mantel-piece; at least they had coal for the fire, so they were warm. They had calmed down by then and saw the funny side of it too, and they could see I was genuinely sorry and was getting it sorted.

I had some real heart-to-heart conversations with Blodwen over the following days about where I was go-ing with my life, what I wanted to do, what we both wanted to do together, and how the fuck I was going to achieve all that. I needed to calm down and sort my shit out if I was going to be a proper boyfriend who could help towards the bills and take Sam on holidays and do proper stuff like other couples do, but I didn't know where to start.

Gis a Job, I can do that

For the next few weeks, my head was all over the place. I slept over Blodwen's house most of the time but I was still doing discos and raving with Rob on the weekends. My stepfather fixed the door but didn't give me a key. He left the back door open for me but I felt it was a subtle sign from him that I needed to get my own place, sort my life out, grow up and get a trade. He knew I was staying with Blodwen a lot and asked me once if I had any plans to move in with her.

I was starting to fall in love with Blodwen and the feeling was mutual; we got on really well and enjoyed being together and finding out about each other. She was just what I needed and she told me I was what she needed, although I couldn't understand why she needed someone like me; I had fuck all to bring to the table. We talked about the future and me getting a job, learning to drive, going on holidays, going out for meals. It frightened the shit out of me, not because I didn't want to do all that, but I didn't know *how* to do it; how to get from where I was to where we wanted to be.

I was sitting in my house one day, all on my own, thinking about all sorts of things, and an old school friend called in to see me. I hadn't seen Julie for years; she'd moved away not long after we all left school. She was a waitress in a Pontins holiday camp in Weymouth and had come home for the week to visit her parents.

I asked her if she could get me a job; I was only joking really but the next day, she called back down to my house and offered me a job as a waiter. Talk about putting your money where your mouth is; I was suddenly faced with a dilemma: I had a job if I wanted one but it meant leaving home and leaving Blodwen. The job was until December because that's when the holiday camp season was over, which meant I would be away for ten months. I would have holidays in between so I could come home if I wanted. It was £75 a week plus tips, which Julie reckoned could take it up to £100 a week. I would have a room of my own, and all meals would be provided; I could eat as much as I wanted because food was on tap, so to speak. So that happened on a Friday but I couldn't give her an answer there and then; I needed to think about it and talk to Blodwen, Rob, and the rest of the boys. She said to let her know by Sunday because she was going back on Monday.

I didn't write as many diary entries back in those days as I should have, but I wrote about this particular time in my life and still have it. So this is from my diary, word for word...

Tuesday 2ⁿᵈ February 1993

I went down Blodwen's, told her that I have a job and I got to go away if I take it, she said to take it otherwise she would blame herself if I didn't, it was a sad night. We talked about it for ages and I still hadn't told the boys, so she said why don't I go over the shed for an hour and see what the boys say. So I did, I went over to the shed, and all the boys were there, and they said go for it, they all thought it was mad, but they said go for it. Anyway I stayed for a while, then went back to Blodwen's. She asked me what did the boys say, I said, they said go for it. That's when she started crying I didn't know what to say I feel as though I have hurt her and that's the last thing I wanted to do, I feel as though I have stepped into her life, let her fall in love with me then I fuck off, I feel a cunt. She said she would wait for me and she would come up and see me. I hope she don't meet anyone else, but in a way I would be glad for her if she did and she was happy, because that's what I want. I want her to be happy, and I hope I don't meet anyone else up there because I love Blodwen and I want to come back to her.

I knew if I wanted to turn my life around, the only way to do it was to move away from everything and everyone, and give myself the space and time to find myself again. I found myself once before so I knew I could do it but this time, I also had to reinvent myself. I could've found a job locally if I put my mind to it but I would still be surrounded by the boys, by Rob and the rave scene, so nothing would change.

I decided to take the job; in my head, I had no choice. So I told Julie the next day and she arranged to pick me up on Monday morning. She told me I needed black trousers, a white shirt and black shoes, and the rest of the uniform would be provided. I had a shirt and trousers but didn't have black shoes. On the Sunday afternoon, I told my stepfather and my brother that I was going away to work in a holiday camp; my stepfather said it was a runaway job but he was happy that I found work and gave me £20, telling me not to fuck it up. He was right, it was a runaway job, but it was something I needed to do. I asked my brother if I could have his black shoes and I would send him the money for them when I got settled in but he said no because he wore them all the time.

I told all the boys I was going; Rob didn't want me to and tried to convince me to stay. He told me we would get more bookings for discos and ease off on the raving but I told him I had made up my mind and needed to get away for my sanity. He said he would give it a month, then I'd be back home.

On the Sunday night I stayed at Blodwen's house. Neither of us slept; we lay in bed, talking and crying all night. I knew I needed to go; I needed to take that job and Blodwen knew it as well. We didn't want to split up, so we vowed to stay together, phone each other every night, and write to each other. I would come home on my holidays, and she could come to Weymouth on her holidays. I needed a clean break from it all to start fresh, I needed four square meals a day and a steady income, but most of all, I needed to sort my head out so I could come back and be a proper boyfriend to Blodwen. I couldn't do all that if I stayed and I knew that for certain; I had to get away from it all. As much as I didn't want to leave Blodwen, a bigger picture was at play for long-term stability.

Hi-De-Hi Campers

On Monday morning, we were still crying. Rob came over to say goodbye and said he would call over to Blodwen's house when I phoned her so we could have a three-way chat. It was really sad. I said goodbye to Sam and told her I would write to her as well, then Julie arrived and off I went. But before I left, I asked her to call to my house. I got in through the back door; nobody was awake. I found my brother's shoes and took them with me, leaving an IOU on the mantelpiece.

It was a three-and-a-half-hour journey to Weymouth and on the way, Julie explained Pontins a little bit more to me. She said it was an adults-only camp, which basically meant it was a holiday camp for old people, but they did close the place down to the public a few times a year for private functions. One was a psychic/medium event where they come from all over the UK to have a convention, and she enjoyed that week the most because she got free psychic readings. Then she went through naming and describing all the staff; from what she told me, the boys in the kitchen sounded like the type of people I would get on with. It was all a bit of an information overload for me. I couldn't stop thinking of Blodwen and wondering if I had made a big mistake.

We finally arrived, then I had to meet everybody. The head waiter was from Merthyr, which was just up the road from where I lived, and the head chef was from Newport, which was not far from Cardiff, where I was born. So there were four people from Wales there altogether, including me. I was right about the kitchen staff; I could tell they were all stoners straight away. My room was small, with a double bed, sink, small wardrobe, TV unit with a portable TV, and a heater on a wall. It was like a prison cell but with no toilet so I had to use the communal toilet and bathroom in the hallway; I knew that I would be using the sink more than the communal toilet, but not for a poo. I didn't even have anything to play music on, although I took my tapes and all my flyers with me.

The first thing I did was put a picture of Blodwen next to the television and then unpacked what little I had, then I lay on the bed and cried, wondering what the fuck I had done. Then I went to the telephone box downstairs to phone Blodwen, pretending everything was okay. When I went back to my room, I picked up my notepad and pen and wrote the following:

I am determined to find myself here in this place. I'm not going to leave until Carlos comes out in me. I've got to find myself. It's like I'm giving myself a challenge.

I wanted to call Rob but he didn't have a phone so I wrote him a letter telling him that I would find myself and he should too while I was away.

My working hours were as follows:

Breakfast shift – 8-10
Lunch shift – 12:30-3
Dinner shift – 6:30-9

Two days off a week based on a rota, meaning I would have to work weekends.

This meant that I wouldn't be able to watch Neighbours at 1:25 but I could catch the repeat at 5:25. When I went to sort out all my details with the secretary, she told me my name was flagged up as owing poll tax; I knew that because there was a warrant out for my arrest for non-payment. I didn't tell her that bit but after a few phone calls, she said they would have to deduct an extra five pounds a week from my wages to pay it off, and I was okay with that; at least it meant the police wouldn't turn up and arrest me. I went on an induction course to learn how to be a waiter and got my Health & Hygiene certificate.

I spoke to Blodwen every night from the payphone downstairs; we'd talk for hours and were writing to each other as well. I bought a little stereo player from one of the boys and put my flyers on the wall to make my room feel less like a prison cell. It turned out that I was a pretty good waiter; it was fast-paced, and I made a few mistakes, but everyone eventually got what they wanted. All the guests loved me and thought I was cute, which always happened with old people, ever since I can remember; they all used to say that I looked like a young Johhny Mathis (for you youngsters out there, he sang "When a Child is Born"). I was getting between £20 and £30 tips a week and Julie was glad that I was getting into it.

The food there was great; I had never had such an abundance of it around me and we had whatever was on the menu for the guests. In the mornings, I'd have a full breakfast with about six rashers of bacon, with a bowl of Alpen to finish it off, and sometimes I would have a kipper. I was really pushing the boat out and getting all exotic with my food. It was the best I had eaten in my life; I gorged like fuck because I needed to put weight on.

Every night after work I would hang around with the kitchen staff; I got on really well with them. We would take it in turns to go to each other's rooms, where we'd drink cider, play cards and get stoned. The boys loved my flyers. They had never been to a rave before and wanted to hear all about the experience; I was happy to tell them and promised to take them all to a big rave one day. I gave them some of my spare flyers and made them all copies of my rave tapes.

On my days off, I would go down to Weymouth or sit in my room all day. After a few months, I felt much more settled and had some spare cash. I sent money to my mate to pay off my monthly instalments of the loan he had for me, and I paid my brother back for his shoes. But I was feeling homesick; I wanted to see Blodwen and I was missing everyone else as well. I had built up some holidays so I booked time off to go back home for five days. I made sure it was a Monday to a Friday so I wouldn't be tempted to go out on the weekend to a rave. I caught the train home and went straight to Blodwen's house. We were both happy as fuck to see each other, and Sam was glad to see me, too; we had a really good night. We stayed up until four in the morning chatting about everything; how we were both feeling, what had been happening, what the future held, and all sorts.

The next day, Rob called over. He had heard I was home somehow and was upset that I didn't tell him and hadn't been to see him; he got over it pretty quickly though. The next few days, I caught up with everyone else; they were surprised that I was sticking it out, and they all agreed that I had put some weight on and looked much healthier. I called over to see my stepfather and the first thing he noticed was that I had put some weight on. He also said he thought I wouldn't be in Pontins for long and was happy that I hadn't quit. The five days went really quickly. There were a few times when I was with Blodwen that I contemplated not going back but I knew that I wasn't ready to stay home for good at that point. Seeing the boys all still doing the same thing made me realise that if I did stay, I would be back into all that straight away. We both cried when we said goodbye.

When I got back to Pontins, Julie was surprised to see me; she didn't think I'd be back but I'd really started settling into life there. Most of the people working there were like me; they were all running away from something or another or hiding from someone or another. I was also starting to feel good about where I was mentally; I had a clear head and a vision for the future. The first things I wanted to do when the season was over was to learn to drive, get a proper job, and go to night school to learn a trade like my stepfather told me I should. I was saving money, I had bought new clothes, I finally paid off the loan my mate had arranged for me, and I didn't have any debts. The tips were really helping to bump up my pay and we would get extra money if the guests had a photograph with us. They would have to buy the photograph and we would get a commission from it. At first, I thought it was a bit cheesy but I could see how much extra money the others were making from it, so I embraced it. I would always ask them if they wanted a picture with me as a memory of their holiday and, truth be told, I became a photo slut.

The week the spiritualists booked the place out was weird; one woman brought her dog with her and said it was her dead husband. They held a mass séance in the ballroom every afternoon and I went to some of them to see what it was all about. Everyone had to be really silent; one of them would sit in the middle of the room and be taken over by a spirit, talking like that girl in "The Exorcist", as if they were possessed. I went home again at the end of April and stayed with Blodwen for a few days; well, it was supposed to be only three days but I stayed for a week. The thing was, when I got back home, all the boys were going to a rave on the Friday, when I was due to travel back. It was a Universe "Tribal Gathering" and Rob was really nagging me to go. He said...

"Come on, Carl, we haven't been to a rave together for ages. It'll be wicked, and it's a Universe as well."

"I can't, Rob. That's the day I'm due to travel back to work."

"Fuck work, mun, phone in sick and go back on Monday. Think of all the fun we'll have; you love a Universe, and everyone else is going as well. It won't be the same without you."

He was right; I did love a Universe rave. I talked to Blodwen about it and, as usual, she said it was up to me what I wanted to do, so I thought fuck it, and I bought a ticket, deciding I would phone in sick and travel back on Monday. I called the boss and told him I had caught a stomach bug.

Tribal Gathering was fucking wicked. Just being in the car park was exciting; everyone was just so happy and friendly and hyped up for it. I did my usual ritual when I got inside and headed straight for the garage tent; it was called "Planet Erotica." I had a little dance in there and then went to explore. There were loads of attractions. I went on the dodgems with random people. It was funny. Normally, whenever I went on the dodgems or "bumper cars", as we used to call them, we would try to bump into each other, but none of us were doing that. We were weaving in and out of each other, making sure we didn't bump the cars; it was very courteous of everyone. There was a fun house too, as well as a ball pool and slides and a crooked bridge. It was like being kids again but without our parents, and it was all free. There were loads of different marquees: Hardcore, Hard House, Garage, and Techno, and people were dancing outside and all around; even outside the toilets. It truly was a full-on party vibe; there were even giant robots walking around. Simon was there as well; it was good to catch up with him. I hadn't seen him for ages and we had a good chat. He was MCing in raves up in Manchester and was loving it up there.

I was walking around in my own world when I heard some wicked music coming from the Techno tent that I just couldn't ignore; it was DJ Tanith. Fuck me, he played a fantastic set that took us all on a cosmic journey. D-Ream were playing in Planet Erotica; I wasn't sure how that would go down because they were a bit mainstream for a rave. I went to listen to them and for the first time ever in a rave, people were singing along to a song:

Things can only get better

Fair play to them, they were perfect. The vocals weren't great but the vibe they brought lifted the place up. I remember thinking, surely things can't get better than this.

On Saturday, I went back to Blodwen's house. I was fucked; the rave had really taken it out of me. I phoned in sick again on Monday and ended up staying home all week, but I knew I had to go back to Pontins. As much as I didn't want to, I knew I wasn't ready yet to stay home.

When I got back, the boys in the kitchen were surprised to see me again; they didn't think they would. That night, we sat in my room and I told them all about Universe; they made me promise that the next Universe rave I went to, I would take them with me. As it happened, a few weeks later, Rob sent me a letter; well, it was four words and a flyer, which was for another Universe rave called "The Time Machine." His four words were...

"You better be there."

The line-up looked amazing. So that night I showed the boys the flyer and told them I was going to take them to their first rave; they were very excited about it indeed. Now, when I say I was going to take them to their first rave, I meant I would organise it all; I couldn't physically take them because I couldn't drive. There were three of them altogether: John was a chef, and Colin and Dean were kitchen porters. I got on really well with them; they were sound as fuck and all around my age as well. John was the only one with a car so he was the designated driver. I told them about my rule of splitting up when we got inside the rave and advised them to do the same; I told them it was a journey they needed to take on their own.

I wrote straight back to Rob with three words…

"I'll be there."

I told Blodwen I was going. I asked her if she wanted to go up with all the boys from the village and meet me there but it wasn't her thing. She told me she probably wouldn't see me all night anyway. She had a good point, mind; I wouldn't know what to do with a girlfriend in a rave. We also arranged for her to come up in July during the school holidays with Sam; there was a holiday park opposite Pontins and I booked a caravan for the week. We were going to have a proper family holiday and I couldn't wait.

A few days before the rave Rob wrote me the following letter:

Well hello there Carl boy, how's yourself? I broke it off with that girl, believe me it was hard, I eventually had the guts to pick up the phone and phone her, oh I was stuttering like fuck, I'm glad I told her I feel much better now. I was in hell of a situation. Anyway I can't wait until Friday, it should be good you better be there, if we haven't seen each other before 12 look for me in the main arena, between 12-4 I'll probably be on the stage having a good time, but you know what we are like, we probably won't see each other all night, but Carl I do want you to look for me, because I will be looking for you and four eyes are better than two, pasta, parsley sauce and scrambled egg. Hi Julie I know you are reading this letter, how are you doing?

Anyway where was I? Oh yeah in my bedroom writing a letter, Oh I will be back now, I'm going to roll a joint. Half an Hour later, hello, another 20 minutes later, oh I couldn't think of anything to write after I said hello, so have another hello, oh believe me I am bricked, I only found out today I was going to Universe, some money just came my way, I was trying to hitch a lift and two fifty pound notes pulled up in this BMW and guess what? They were going my way, so that's how I am going to Universe.Oh two blokes knocked on my door the other day, they were selling double glazing, they asked me if I wanted any fitted in my house, I told them no thanks not today. Anyway I can't remember if I have told you and if I have then tough shit I'm going to tell you again, I'm collecting teddy bears and I've already got 12 so when you come home next rescue a teddy and bring it with you and you can give it to the R.S.P.T.B, Robert's Society for the Protection of Teddy Bears. So Julie any old teddies?

My sponsor and the organisers of my fund especially me will be most grateful. Anyway I think it's time for me to go now, I think I need some kip, well I don't really need a kip but I just love kipping, it's the business. So see you on Friday(hopefully)

Take care brother.

PS. Oh I had to write PS because a letter doesn't sound right without a PS, so this should sound alright now.

Anyway, the day finally arrived for Universe. It was only an hour and a half drive from Weymouth so we left about five o'clock; the boys were excited as fuck and hyper as well. When we arrived, we met up with Rob and everyone else, and bought our refreshments. Rob fucked off to find a weak spot in the security while the rest of us queued up. My stomach was in knots. I gave the boys a little pep talk about drinking plenty of water and going into the chill-out room if they needed a break. When we got through the gates, I hugged them and told them to take care, and off I skipped to the portaloo to empty my excited bowels. I turned around to check on them and make sure they weren't still standing there like kids being dropped off in the playground, and I watched as the three of them split up in different directions. They certainly took my advice to the letter; they were boys after my own heart, bless them.

I caught up with each one of them a few times throughout the night. John was walking around, hand in handwith a girl he had met at the fun fair; he said he loved her, he loved me, he loved the Universe, and he loved life. I was glad to see he was loving it; he spent all night with that girl.

I danced with Colin in the garage tent; he was a garage head like me and a good dancer. He said the music hit him deep in his soul and I was glad to see him feeling it.

Dean was chilling out on the grass by the bouncy castle most of the night, getting stoned, meeting people and taking in all the sights and sounds, of which there were plenty. He liked the music but he preferred to meet people and chat; he was a proper stoner that way. There was also a circus arena, with trapeze artists, tightrope walkers, fire breathers, acrobats, and a cinema; I went in there and sat on the bean bags. I caught up with Rob, who had managed to sneak in; he said he just walked through the gates and nobody asked him for a ticket. We had a good chat about things; what he wanted to do with his life, and what I wanted to do. He was feeling the same as me, that he needed a break from it all as well, but didn't know

301

how to go about it; he was still doing discos but they were wearing him down.

The morning came and we were in the car park saying goodbye to everyone. I don't know why I did it, but I turned to Rob and said...

"Do you fancy coming back to Weymouth with us for a little holiday? You'll have a place to stay and all the food you can eat for a week."

"Are you serious?"

"Yes. One of the Bluecoats left last week; I'll ask the boss if you can stay in his room. He won't mind; he's cool like that, and you could do with a break."

John, Colin and Dean all thought it was a good idea too; they liked Rob and thought he was a good laugh. So he agreed and we took him back to Pontins with us. When we got back, I asked the boss if it was okay for Rob to stay in the spare room; he was fine with it as long as it was only a week. Blodwen was surprised when I phoned and told her Rob was staying for the week, and she went a bit quiet for a while; I think that was the first time I had pissed her off.

Anyway, it was good to have Rob around. I had to work but he kept himself busy, getting stoned and eating food. He got on with all the boys, and they all thought he was nuts... because he was. I had two days off in the middle of the week so we went down to Weymouth for a drink and to the local nightclub. He liked Weymouth, and Pontins too; he was enjoying the break. We were all sat in my room one night when John mentioned that one of the other kitchen porters had left so they were a K.P. down. He looked over to Rob and said...

"Do you want a job as a kitchen porter?"

"What do I have to do?"

"Wash pots and pans, that's all; it's really easy."

We all discussed it for a while. I wasn't sure it was a good idea to have Rob up there with me all the time; I might end up going to raves on the weekends and I didn't want to get back into all that. The occasional big rave now and then was okay but not every weekend. It was good to see him for a week and have him around, but I didn't know if I could handle him being there all the time; I didn't have strong enough willpower to say no if he wanted to go out partying. But he liked the idea and said he would try it out for two weeks. If he got into it, he would go home, get his decks, and set them up in his room; the boys loved that idea.

I wasn't sure about it but luckily, he only ended up staying for two weeks. He hated the job; he was stuck in a steamy little room in the kitchen scrubbing pots and pans, and the head chef took a dislike to him because he wouldn't listen to his instructions or do as he was told. He also had to do his hygiene certificate; in the history of Pontins, nobody had ever failed it. Rob managed that feat though; he had to sit it twice because he was stoned all the time and not paying attention. After one of his shifts in the kitchen, he came running through the busy restaurant, straight out through the doors, and jumped into the swimming pool, fully clothed, in front of some guests. The boss was not happy about that at all, and neither was I; staff weren't allowed in the pool when guests were in there, especially not in full uniform.

The other thing he used to do was sing at the top of his voice as he was washing pots and pans. The chef didn't like that either because people in the kitchen couldn't hear the orders being shouted out, and every time the door swung open, everyone in the restaurant could hear him as well. The head waiter told him to shut up a few times and I told him off about it as well; said he was embarrassing me. But he didn't give a fuck about things like that; he just thought I was being stupid for feeling embarrassed over something someone else was doing.

He asked me if I could get him a job as a waiter in the restaurant so I asked the boss. His words were…

"I don't mind him working in the kitchen but I don't want him anywhere near the guests."

So in the end, he went back home. I was glad, he was glad, the head chef, the boss, and Blodwen were all glad. Before he left, he made a point of going to see the head chef and apologising to him; they shook hands and laughed about it. I was happy to see him go; he was really stressing me out. It was like looking after a petulant child, having him around.

July finally arrived and Blodwen and Sam came up for the week. Her stepfather and mother brought them up, so we all went for a meal together and then they left us to it. I was so excited to see them. I introduced her to everyone and showed her my humble abode; she was a bit shocked at my pokey little room.

We had a lovely caravan in the holiday park, with its clubhouse and adventure playground. It felt a bit weird at first to be all responsible, like a father, and have a proper family but I soon got over that. We took Sam to the Sea Life Adventure park, played mini golf, went to the fair, and visited Monkey World. One of the nights, Julie babysat for Sam, so we went out clubbing; we had a great time together as a family. When it was time to leave, her stepfather came to pick them up. We were all crying, saying goodbye; I could have just said fuck it and gone home with them but I still wasn't ready.

In August, Universe were doing their last rave of the year, called "Big Love". It was on a Friday, the 13th, and it was a twenty-four-hour rave, starting at 12 midday Friday and finishing the same time on Saturday. When I read the flyer, I knew I had to go:

"Big Love" will be the gathering to take the large-scale outdoor dance party back to basics, back to its roots and the old-skool vibe, and forward to a positive, brighter future by cementing the spirit that binds us all together, whatever our dance music persuasion. We will be inviting all generations to unite, harmonise, and dispel negative attitudes and acknowledge membership of the global dance community and the energy it represents.

The hardcore tent was called "Earth", the garage tent was called "Heaven", and D.I.Y Sound System were there as well. Plus, of course, a fun fair. Colin couldn't make it because he wasn't allowed the time off but John and Dean came with me. John was the only one with transport so I was glad he could make it. Once again, Universe lived up to expectations; I was in "Heaven" most of the night and then went over to "Earth" to listen to the Prodigy and Top Buzz. The best set of the night for me was Paul Oakenfold; it was proper hard house and funky as fuck. Every time a bit of piano music came on, I was rushing my box off; I fucking love piano and was in my element.

I still enjoy listening to that set on YouTube. It was the first twenty-four-hour rave I had been to and it was a bit of a struggle to get through it; I needed plenty of refreshments. I caught up with Rob, who had climbed over the fence to get in. Security chased him but he lost them in the hardcore tent. He ended up on stage when Carl Cox played his set. I didn't know it at the time but "Big Love" happened to be the last big outdoor rave that I went to, and to be honest with you, I couldn't have chosen a better one.

Blodwen came to Weymouth for the weekend in September; it was lovely to spend time on our own. We went out for meals, took a walk up the mountain, sat on the beach watching the sunset, and went out clubbing. I was feeling really good about myself and our situation. Things were looking up and I was feeling more comfortable about who I was. I could see a light at the end of the tunnel and a bright future for us.

In October, I really knuckled down, not going out anywhere because I knew I was on the last leg of my running away journey. I wanted to save as much money as I could for Christmas and to take home. I make it sound like I was in some sort of prison and couldn't escape. I could have left anytime but I wanted to stick the whole season out. I needed to prove to myself that I could commit to something and not quit. All my life had been disruptive because I'd had no control over it, but now I did. I needed to prove to myself that if I say I am going to do something, I will do it and stay the course.

Sometime in October, on a Sunday afternoon, I was lying on my bed between shifts when one of the Bluecoats knocked on my door and told me that five boys were in the reception area asking for me. I wasn't expecting anyone, especially five people. I thought it was a wind-up, but there really were five boys in reception asking for me; it was some of my mates from back home. They all looked fucked; they had been to Obsession in Cornwall Coliseum and, thinking Weymouth wasn't far from there, they decided to pop in and see me.

Weymouth was a two-and-a-half-hour drive from Cornwall and it took them four hours to find me; they could have driven home in that time. They told me they had even driven down the wrong side of the motorway after coming out of the services; it was lucky the roads were quiet as fuck at that time of the morning. I took them all to my room; they weren't very talkative and looked a bit traumatised. I went downstairs to the kitchen to plate them all up a roast dinner. I piled loads on the plate for them because they looked like they needed a good meal, but none of them could eat it. I even asked if they wanted something from the salad bar but they didn't want any of that either; I should have known, really. They stayed for a few hours; I think they needed a little rest. It was good to see them, even though I couldn't get a decent conversation out of any of them.

The end of the season arrived and it was time to go home. I had managed to save just over a thousand pounds, the most money I had ever had in my life, and I bought loads of Christmas presents for Blodwen and Sam. I had put weight on, saved money, and found myself. All the boxes were ticked and I was ready to go back home to Blodwen. It was sad saying goodbye to everyone. Obviously, I wrote down people's addresses to write to them and told all the boys they were welcome to visit Wales anytime. I was going to miss them; we had built up a good friendship, working and playing together every day for almost a year. We said we would keep in touch and maybe even see each other in raves; they were all fully-fledged ravers by the time I left. Julie gave me a lift because she was going home for Christmas.

All in all, running away to join a holiday camp did me a world of good. I needed that space to detach myself from everyone, even though it was hard because every day, I missed Blodwen. But it was a means to an end; it was necessary.

Anyway, that about wraps up my story and my book, apart from the epilogue, which I'll keep short and sweet.

Epilogue

This is the bit where I wrap it all up and, to be honest with you, I never thought I would finish this book. I have been working on it, on and off, for decades so first of all, I would like to thank you if you managed to get to the end. I hope you enjoyed my journey and maybe it might have even inspired you to write your own stories of those hazy, crazy days.

When I arrived home after Pontins, I went straight to Blodwen's house and never left. I learned to drive; it took me two attempts to pass my test, and Rob reckoned I would *never* pass it. I got a job working in a factory and went to night school to learn a trade, just like my stepfather told me to. I became a website designer for a while and then I went into IT support. I had a job with the council, working in schools as an IT Support Officer, and now I work for a software company. In my spare time, I also make videos on social media; I call them comedy but comedy is subjective. I also teach people how to use social media.

Ten years after I met Blodwen, we went back to Weymouth to get married. We are still together and have two more children. Sam has just turned 40 and has a little boy of her own.

Simon and his girlfriend split up but he is now happily married and has a big family.

Me and Rob are still very close friends. We have had our arguments over the years but our friendship is as solid as ever and we haven't had a disagreement for about a decade now. I spoke to him last night and he told me to tell you that he is happy in himself spiritually.

I don't go raving anymore, and I know that this might be a bone of contention for some but for me personally, the rave scene wasn't the same after 1993, and neither was I. But I am glad to see that hardcore never died and is still going strong, and lately, there has been a massive revival taking place, which spurred me on to finish my book. I do have a few more stories but I couldn't fit them all in this book; well, I could, but I needed to stop somewhere, so maybe I'll write another, shorter book with all my poems and miscellaneous stories.

And if you want to see more of what I get up to in my spare time I am on TikTok and Facebook. Just search for "Carlosmanwelly."

Take care you lovely lot and thank you very much.

Be cheerful. Strive to be happy.

Printed in Great Britain
by Amazon

58685076R00178